Babci's Chicken Soup (page 71)

P9-DXQ-786

About The Authors

Elaine Groen and Irene Rapp are Registered Dietitians practicing in the San Francisco bay area. They have been involved in food management and nutrition education for over 10 years. They are members of the American Dietetic Association and co-authors of the "Successfully Slim" weekly newspaper column offering practical information and tips on how to develop a healthier way of eating. As working mothers they understand the need for preparing good food in a hurry. This book is their non-technical answer to the need for a collection of creative, healthy recipes that can be prepared quickly.

At last — A handy collection of healthy and delicious recipes you can prepare in a hurry.

- Authored by two well-known San Francisco Registered Dietitians, Elaine Groen and Irene Rapp.
- Not overly restrictive or another "diet" book — a ready reference of delicious, everyday recipes for sensible, healthy eating.
- Fresh vegetables, fruits, salads, cheese, fish and chicken dishes abound!
- Cooking times and time-saving tips for those owning a microwave, food processor or blender.
- For easy use, this book lies flat when opened, contains one recipe per page and is printed in large easy-to-read type.
- Compact design—takes a minimum of counter space.

*To John, Melanie, Gretchen and Rachel
who supported us and taste-tested
many a recipe, and to Dennis whose
help was boundless.*

Healthy Cooking
on the run

by
Elaine Groen R.D.
Irene Rapp R.D.

©Copyright 1983
Nitty Gritty Productions
P.O. Box 5457
Concord, California 94524-0457

A Nitty Gritty Cookbook
Printed by Mariposa Press
Concord, California

All rights reserved. This book or any part
thereof may not be reproduced without the
written permission of the publisher.

Library of Congress Catalog Card
Number, 83-061791
ISBN 0-911954-75-9

2nd Printing

Editor: Jackie Walsh
Art Director: Mike Nelson
Illustrator: Dorothy Davis
Photographer: Bruce Henson
Food Stylist: Cherie Miller

Special thanks to **The Kitchen** (Berkeley, CA)
and to **Zebra** (Berkeley, CA) for the cookware
and props in our photographs.

Table of Contents

Introduction

Interest in nutrition is skyrocketing. We now understand the role of diet in preventing illness, reducing stress and promoting a healthy lifestyle. There is no lack of information about proper nutrition, however much of it is complicated or controversial.

Many popular magazines regularly print articles about nutrition and weight control. Vitamins and minerals are heavily advertised. Talk shows regularly feature "nutritionists" who present varying points of view about nutrition.

Because of all of the publicity, many people feel that nutrition means handfuls of vitamins and minerals, unusual ingredients, or foods that taste dreadful! (If you do not eat your sea kelp and alfalfa, how can you be healthy?)

Most people are feeding their families properly. We hope that this book will reinforce the positive contributions that you make toward your health. We hope that you will also be aided in your efforts by our information.

Consumers are learning of the values of tasty whole grains, legumes and the delectable variety of fresh produce available in their markets. Many cooks are drawn to "cooking from scratch," yet few of us have the time, or even the desire, to spend long hours in the kitchen preparing a meal that will be devoured in a few minutes!

As nutritionists, we want you to know that good nutritious recipes can:

- taste delicious
- use many of your favorite ingredients
- be prepared quickly and easily

Our clients over the years have repeatedly asked us for an easy-to-follow cookbook of wholesome and nutritious recipes. They have requested recipes that are appealing to both adults and children and make use of familiar ingredients.

This book is in response to these requests. All recipes utilize the "Secrets of Healthy Eating" (page 21), and we have included tips for transforming *your* own favorite recipes to improve nutrition, while preserving flavor.

By using the recipes in Healthy Cooking on the Run, you will be assured of serving meals that are healthy, wholesome and appealing!

Modern Nutrition Basics
BALANCE, VARIETY AND MODERATION

Our American diet is essentially good. Americans live longer than the people of other nations. We are taller and have fewer diseases than preceding generations. We have a wide variety of abundant foods. Even American favorites, such as cheeseburgers, meat loaf and spaghetti, are healthy and wholesome.

Yet, all is not well. Most of the fatal illnesses in our country are nutrition-related. Poor eating habits can contribute to heart disease, stroke, kidney disease, cancer, diabetes and obesity. It is time to "modernize" our menus to gain better nutrition while eliminating harmful and unnecessary ingredients.

Good nutrition is composed of: Balance, Variety and Moderation. We have used these three elements in deriving our Secrets Of Healthy Eating which are described in a later chapter.

BALANCE YOUR NUTRITION
AS YOU BALANCE YOUR CHECKBOOK

To assure a well-balanced diet, we need to select foods each day from the four basic food groups: (1) Dairy Products, (2) Meat, Fish, Poultry and Eggs, (3) Fruits and Vegetables, (4) Grains, Breads and Cereals.

Each of these groups contains "leader" (most important) nutrients. They are: (1) calcium, (2) protein, (3) vitamins A and C and (4) B-complex vitamins. It is difficult to receive the full quota of "leader" nutrients, plus other nutrients closely associated with the "leaders," unless we balance our diets by selecting foods from each group.

The number of daily servings from each group necessary to provide a balanced diet is easy to remember with this formula: For an adult 2-2-4-4 handles it! This refers to *2 servings* from Group (1); *2 servings* from Group (2); *4 servings* from Group (3); and *4 servings* from Group (4). For children, the formula is 3-2-4-4 and for adolescents, 4-4-4-4. These servings may be eaten anytime during the day.

Remember, 2-2-4-4 is the key to a balanced diet for adults. Just one formula for a lifetime.

THE EASY WAY TO A BALANCED DIET

The Four Basic Food Groups

1. DAIRY
(milk, yogurt, cheese)

"Leader" nutrient:
Calcium

Other important
nutrients:
Riboflavin
Protein

One serving =
8 ounces milk or
    yogurt
1 ounce cheese

2. PROTEIN
(meat, fish, poultry, eggs)

"Leader" nutrient:
Protein

Other important
nutrients:
Vitamin B$_{12}$
Iron

One serving =
2 to 3 ounces

**3. VEGETABLES
    & FRUITS**

"Leader" nutrients:
Vitamins A and C

Other important
nutrients:
Potassium
Fiber

One serving =
½ cup

4. GRAINS
(bread, cereals)

"Leader" nutrients:
B-complex Vitamins

Other important
nutrients:
Minerals
Fiber

One serving =
½ cup cereal
1 slice bread

There is more to dietary balance than just meeting nutrient needs. Balance also means NOT overindulging in one kind of food at the expense of another.

In the United States in the past years, the value of protein has been overemphasized while carbohydrates have often been criticized. Meat does contain good quality protein, iron and zinc. However, it is a high-fat, high-calorie, low-fiber food, and in the average diet it is often out of balance with other foods. It isn't necessary to eliminate meat, we simply need to reduce the portions. It is surprising how much pasta, vegetables, fruit and milk you can add to replace the excess meat in a meal. For example, you can **EITHER** eat:

8 ozs. of steak   **OR**

3 ozs. of steak PLUS:
1 cup pasta
½ cup green peas
2 slices French bread with 1 tsp. margarine
green salad with 1 tbs. Italian dressing
1 cup strawberries
8 ozs. low-fat milk

By keeping a food journal, you can easily see how well-balanced your diet is. The foods most often missing are whole grains, fruits, vegetables and milk. Try an experiment for yourself. Jot down what you eat each day for several days and see if you are getting your 2-2-4-4 balance.

VARIETY IS THE SPICE OF LIFE

Nature supplies us with a glorious array of food. With improved production, transportation and storage, all parts of our country can share a wide variety of foods. No other country has such abundance, so easily available.

Healthy, good tasting, nutritious foods are the most natural and least expensive means of obtaining the nutrients our bodies need. We don't have to gulp pills and sprinkle powders when we can eat nutrients in their "natural" form.

Variety is a necessary adjunct to balance because it IS possible to eat from all of the food groups and still not ingest all of the needed nutrients. Some foods in each group are richer sources for certain nutrients than others. For example, if all of your dairy servings were eaten as cottage cheese, calcium would be lacking because cottage cheese isn't as rich a source of calcium as milk or yogurt. If all of your fruits and vegetables were apples, carrots and celery, your vitamin C intake would be compromised.

By eating a large variety of foods from each of the four groups, you ensure a plentiful supply of all nutrients.

"MODERNIZE" BY MODERATION

It's been said that the major American nutritional problem is overeating. We consume too many calories, eat too much meat, use too much salt and sugar, and drink too much alcohol and caffeine. Our excesses contribute to the alarming health statistics on cardiovascular diseases, obesity, diabetes and cancer.

It would be just as wrong to totally remove these foods from our diets. What we should do is to identify the excesses in our diets and work consistently to reduce them.

What goes into our mouths goes first into our shopping carts, so it makes sense to correct our shopping habits. Place fewer salted items, meats and carbonated beverages in your shopping cart, and replace them with wholesome grains, fresh produce and milk.

Another area in which we can "lighten up" is in our cooking. We can learn to substitute other ingredients to obtain flavorful recipes without excess salt, fat and calories. All of the recipes in this book have been chosen for good taste and nutrition.

Dining out is the third place for us to correct our habits. We can order lighter meals and request that high-fat items be served "on the side," and we can let our feelings be known to the establishment about salty soups and sauces.

Be sure to allow yourself your favorite foods occasionally. Buy one small bag of potato chips rather than 3 large bags. Cut down on chocolate and other sweets. Serve steak less often, or cut your portion in half. Eat it slowly and savor each morsel. Discover which favorite foods are nutritionally wholesome and serve them more often. Balance, Variety and Moderation form the basis of our Secrets To Healthy Eating.

Five Secrets to Healthy Eating

Take time to study your present food intake. You probably enjoy a fairly nutritious diet. It may need only a few modifications to make it healthier.

SECRET NUMBER ONE:
EAT MORE COMPLEX CARBOHYDRATES

For years diet books have been telling us to eliminate carbohydrates. Sugars and starches are lumped together as "fat-makers." Potato? Forget it! Pasta? Too fattening! How about corn? Too much starch!

At last, nutritionists are fighting back—and loudly enough for all to hear! Carbohydrates are rich sources of B-vitamins, minerals, such as zinc and magnesium, and fiber. And they are very low in calories.

It will be more helpful to distinguish between sources of carbohydrates. **Simple carbohydrates** are the sugars—sugar (sucrose), dextrose (glucose), fructose, honey, corn syrup, molasses, lactose (milk sugar) and fruits. These carbohydrates are easily absorbed by the body and are used for "quick" energy. Like all foods, any excess will be stored as fat.

Since your body's energy source is glucose (like gasoline for your car), there is nothing inherently wrong with eating sugars. They are NOT poisons. However, foods containing sugar often carry few other nutrients. It is easy for us to eat these "nutrient-poor" foods instead of "nutrient-dense" foods.

The exception to lack of nutrients in sugar-containing foods is fruit. The carbohydrates in fruits are the simple sugars, glucose and fructose, yet fruits can be rich sources of vitamins, minerals and fiber. Because of the water content, these "natural beauties" are also low in calories.

Complex carbohydrates, on the other hand, are composed of long strings of sugar molecules. Your body takes time to digest and absorb these. Complex carbohydrate foods contain varying amounts of protein and are rich sources of vitamins and minerals.

By choosing whole grains and legumes from this group of foods, you also increase your daily intake of fiber. Many researchers now believe that fiber and other roughage have a preventative effect against diseases of the bowel, such as diverticulosis, spastic colon and bowel cancers.

Complex carbohydrate foods (especially whole grains, vegetables and legumes) offer low calories **plus** good nutrition! In addition, fewer calories are absorbed due to a speedier gastrointestinal transit time. You feel lighter, you feel better and you feel more satisfied with your meals.

Eat More "Complex" Carbohydrates

"SIMPLE"
CARBOHYDRATES

Sugar
Honey
Molasses
Candy
Fruit
Fruit Juices
Soft Drinks
Icings

"COMPLEX"
CARBOHYDRATES

Cereal
Pasta
Rice
Bread
Potatoes
Dried beans and peas
   (legumes)
Vegetables
Starches

SECRET NUMBER TWO:
EAT MORE FRUITS AND VEGETABLES

Fresh fruits and vegetables provide us with crunchy, tasty, pleasing, colorful foods to go with otherwise monotonous meat and grains. They offer a marvelous variety of tastes and smells. Yet fruits and vegetables are often excluded from our daily diets because they require an "extra step" in meal preparation. We would reach for carrot sticks if they were available, already washed and sliced. Since they are not, potato chips get the nod. Lunch tends to be a hot dog and a coke—no vegetables or fruit; dinner often includes a cooked vegetable or salad, but fruit is overlooked.

Low-fat, low-calorie fruits and vegetables can be dressed up, or dressed down. What is more satisfying than a thick, hot vegetable soup on a cold wintry day, or the icy juiciness of a fresh peach or orange on a warm summer day?

Best of all, these choice foods offer excellent nutrition. "Leader" nutrients include vitamins A and C, as well as potassium and fiber.

Most of us naturally think of citrus when vitamin C is mentioned. However, other fruits and vegetables also contain large doses of this important vitamin. You don't have to gulp vitamin C tablets—you can get it the tasty way. With the variety of foods available, it is easy to include a small amount of vitamin C with every meal. For example: breakfast—orange sections; lunch—coleslaw; dinner—potatoes.

Busy Day Stew (page 131) ▶

The symptoms of vitamin A excess or deficiency are similar. It can be harmful to supplement your diet with megadoses of this vitamin. If you haven't been eating fruits and vegetables for a very long period of time, perhaps you may need to re-introduce high-vitamin A foods daily (see chart). Otherwise, every other day is sufficient.

Rich Sources of Vitamins A, C and Potassium

VITAMIN A		VITAMIN C		POTASSIUM	
Fruits	Vegetables	Fruits	Vegetables	Fruits	Vegetables
apricots	asparagus	cactus	broccoli	apricots	artichokes
cantaloupe	avocados	cantaloupe	cabbage	bananas	avocados
cherries	beans—green	cassaba	cauliflower	cantaloupes	beans—lima
elderberries	broccoli	grapefruit	potatoes	dates	broccoli
grapefruit—pink	brussel sprouts	honeydew		oranges	carrots
kumquats	carrots	kiwi		papayas	greens—all
mandarin oranges	corn—yellow	lemons		persimmons	parsnips
papayas	greens—all	limes		pomegranates	peas—split or
peaches	okra	mango		prunes	black-eyed
persimmons	parsley	papaya		raisins	peppers—chili
prunes	peas	strawberries		tangelos	potatoes
tangerines	peppers—green	tangelo		tomatoes	radishes
tomatoes	pumpkins	tangerines		watermelons	winter squash
watermelons	rutabagas	watermelon (all)			sweet potatoes
	squashes				yams
	sweet potatoes				

Anyone taking diuretics on the advice of a physician has probably been advised to maintain an adequate potassium intake. Many fruits and vegetables are natural sources of this mineral (see chart on page 24) and taste much better than a supplement.

Fruits and vegetables contain a wide variety of nutrients in varying amounts, and these foods also provide needed bulk and fiber. Some of the roughage is unseen, as is the indigestible pectin in foods such as apples, pears, bananas and peas.

It is a myth that fruits and vegetables from modern farms are lacking in nutrients. Just as certain nutrients are needed for our development, so does an orange, for example, need all its nutrients to become an orange. If those nutrients are unavailable, the orange will not develop, or will develop so weakly as to be unedible and unmarketable.

The choice of cooking methods also determines what nutrients are maintained. Nutrients can be saved by steaming, microwaving or cooking quickly in small amounts of water. Nutrient loss often depends on surface exposure—the more surface exposed, the more nutrients will be lost (see chart below). Always store fruits and vegetables covered—otherwise, vitamin C, especially, is easily lost.

Nutrients Are Destroyed When Exposed To Air And Water

The More Surface Exposed, The More Nutrients Lost

Potato With Skin
(protected against loss
of nutrients)

Potato Quartered
(much more surface exposed,
more nutrients lost)

Potato Without Skin
(complete outside surface exposed,
many more nutrients lost)

French Fries
(potato completely exposed,
most nutrients quickly lost)

SECRET NUMBER THREE:
EAT LESS SALT

There is a correlation between excess sodium intake and high blood pressure (hypertension), and salt is our main source of sodium. Consequently, lowering salt intake reduces blood pressure. Salt is sodium and chloride, which are necesary for our metabolic functioning, but most Americans eat more salt than they need. Our average intake is one to four teaspoons per day, but our daily requirement is about one-tenth of a teaspoon! Because the symptoms of high blood pressure so often go unnoticed, it is considered prudent for all to reduce the amount of salt in their diet.

It may be helpful to reduce sodium intake gradually. First, identify your major sources of sodium and how much you use (see chart on page 28). Studies show that one-fourth of sodium in the average diet comes naturally in foods, one-fourth is added at the table, and one-half comes from highly-processed, cured and fast foods. Take an inventory and decide where it's easiest to cut down—cured foods, fast foods or at the table.

Experiment with fresh herbs, spices, wine and lemon juice as substitutes for the decreased salt in your diet. Also, try Angostura Bitters, curry powder and dill weed to add flavor to foods that may otherwise seem "flat" at first. Wine is great in chicken dishes, lemon juice perks up vegetables, fish and turkey; fresh parsley, garlic and

A Guideline For Selecting Low-Sodium Foods
Who are the "Good Guys"?

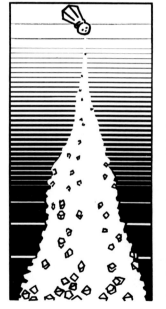

apples,
bananas, oranges
grapefruit
broccoli, green beans
cauliflower, tomatoes

oatmeal, shredded wheat
puffed wheat
rice, noodles
macaroni, spaghetti

clams, shrimp

fish, beef
pork, lamb, poultry

milk
corn niblets

white or wheat bread
cheddar cheese
Swiss cheese

water-packed tuna
ham, bran flakes

hard roll, buttermilk
crab
salted peanuts

luncheon meats
pizza, frankfurters
creamed cottage cheese

canned tomato soup
chow mein

TV dinner

dill pickles

oregano add zest to stews and other combination dishes. Many recipes in this book use dried herbs. Herbs are more flavorful if they are finely crushed, either by rubbing between your fingers or with a mortar and pestle.

Read labels carefully. Watch for the words salt, sodium (as in monosodium glutamate) and soda. You will find them in most processed and packaged foods. Try the new salt-free vegetable and tomato products.

Salt is used in small amounts in some of this book's recipes where we felt a small amount was needed. However, most of the recipes are salt-free. Those who are "heavy salters" may find some of the recipes too "flat" at first. Experiment—add only enough salt to make the food taste good to you, but less than you would usually use. Keep track of how often you shake the salt shaker, then reduce that number gradually.

Modify your favorite recipes by cutting the salt in half and adding different herbs and spices. Your need for the taste of salt will gradually diminish.

SECRET NUMBER FOUR:
EAT LESS SUGAR

Sugar is a natural ingredient used by the body for energy, but statistics show that Americans, on the average, consume more than 100 pounds of sugar each year. We are not suggesting that sugar be eliminated from everyone's diet, but moderation should be practiced.

A few years ago we were told that sugar causes hyperactivity in kids; now we have a study showing that it has a calming effect, rather than a disturbing one.

The real problem arises when highly-sugared foods begin to replace nutritious foods. For example, a coke and candy bar, eaten for lunch or a quick pick-me-up, offers empty calories without nutritional value. The sensation of quick energy after a high-sugar snack is usually followed by an anxious or letdown feeling.

Look at your food intake and identify the major sources of sugar. You need not eliminate it, just cut down on the amount used. Once again, make changes slowly. Read labels and watch for the words sucrose (table sugar), maltose, dextrose, fructose, corn syrup and honey. Use less of these in your daily menus. Kids love snacks such as muffins and granola. They are sweet, yet have far less sugar than cupcakes and they contain other nutritious ingredients such as dried fruits, grains, nuts and

  Barbecued Hamburgers (page 124) ▶

seeds. Try making your own granola with less sugar, serve more milk and yogurt desserts, and buy canned fruits packed in their own juice, rather than syrup.

Avoid Empty Calories, Enjoy Nutritious Meals

EMPTY CALORIES

NUTRITIOUS MEAL

12-ounce cola drink	150 calories		140 calories	2 slices bread
candy bar	300 calories		150 calories	2 ozs. meat, fish or eggs
			45 calories	1 tsp. mayonnaise
			40 calories	small fresh fruit
			90 calories	4 ozs. lowfat milk
	450 calories		**465 calories**	

We have used some sugar in our recipes, but amounts are reduced. When modifying your favorite recipes, try cutting sugar by ⅓ to ½. Use fruit juice, cinnamon, nutmeg and cloves as sweeteners.

Excess sugar is related to dental caries and obesity, so be on the lookout for the culprits. Here are a few:

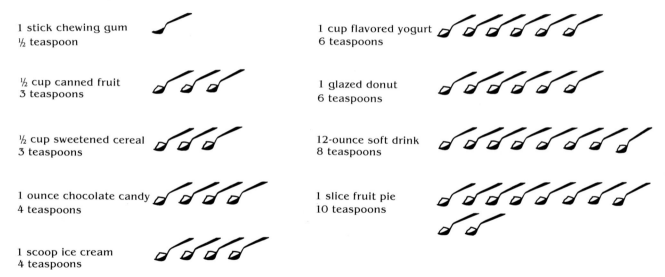

1 stick chewing gum
½ teaspoon

1 cup flavored yogurt
6 teaspoons

½ cup canned fruit
3 teaspoons

1 glazed donut
6 teaspoons

½ cup sweetened cereal
3 teaspoons

12-ounce soft drink
8 teaspoons

1 ounce chocolate candy
4 teaspoons

1 slice fruit pie
10 teaspoons

1 scoop ice cream
4 teaspoons

SECRET NUMBER FIVE: EAT LESS FAT

Fat creeps into our diet so easily and unexpectedly that most of us eat more fat than we realize. Some fat serves a purpose by supplying needed fatty acids, transporting the fat-soluble vitamins (A, D, E and K) to the body tissues, insulating the body, and increasing the sense of satisfaction we feel after eating. By eating less fat, we can reduce caloric intake, maintain body weight and feel more energetic.

Consider this typical breakfast. Over half the total calories are fat calories. Observe how easily the calories can be reduced.

Cooking with Non-Stick Cookware Can Reduce Fat

TYPICAL BREAKFAST	Total Calories	Fat Calories			Total Calories	Fat Calories	LOW–FAT BREAKFAST
					40	0	½ cup orange juice
½ cup orange juice	40	0			156	99	2 eggs fried in non-stick pan
2 eggs, fried in butter	216	154					
3 strips bacon	147	121			65	38	1 slice Canadian bacon
½ cup fried potatoes	229	105			124	0	½ cup potatoes fried in non-stick pan
2 slices buttered toast	230	90			120	0	2 slices toast
					36	36	1 teaspoon butter
	862	**470**			**541**	**173**	

Fats do contribute flavor to foods. Without fat, protein foods would be so tasteless that we wouldn't eat them, yet it only takes a small amount of fat to ensure palatability.

Some fat is "visible" as in butter, margarine, mayonnaise, salad dressings and the fat in meat; however, much is "hidden" as in fried foods, gravies, meats, whole milk, cheese, nuts and avocado! It is especially "unnoticed" in dessert items such as cake, pastries, ice cream and cookies.

We usually think of sweets as being high-sugar foods, but these items may get half of their calories from fat.

For Instance These High-Sugar Foods Are Also High Fat Foods

	Total Calories	Fat Calories		Total Calories	Fat Calories
1 homemade chocolate brownie	146	89	½ cup vanilla ice cream	189	94
1 chocolate chip cookie	57	30	1 small Danish roll	148	74

How To Identify Different Types Of Fat

To make it easier to differentiate types of fat, they are divided into three groups: saturated, unsaturated and cholesterol.

(1) **Saturated fats** are found in both animal and plant foods. Meat fat, lard, butter, coconut oil and palm oil are examples of saturated fats. They are usually solid at room temperature. Some saturated fats contain cholesterol and some do not, yet each of them contributes to higher blood cholesterol levels. Although there is some controversy as to whether elevated blood cholesterol increases risk of heart disease and strokes, most physicians consider it prudent to reduce cholesterol and saturated fat.

(2) **Unsaturated fats** are always from plant sources and are usually liquid at room temperature. They are divided into two groups:
(a) **Polyunsaturated fats** which act as little brooms by sweeping excess cholesterol from blood vessels. Polyunsaturated fats actually reduce blood cholesterol levels and should be the ones most often used. The best sources are corn, safflower and sunflower oils, followed by cottonseed, sesame and soy oils.

(b) **Monosaturated fats** have no effect on blood cholesterol levels. Examples are olive and peanut oils.

(3) **Cholesterol** is a natural body constituent. It is manufactured by the body and has several important functions. Unfortunately, in some people, the body either makes too much or cannot eliminate the excess. Cholesterol accumulates in blood vessels where it begins to clog the vessels and restrict blood flow. Cholesterol is only found in "animal" tissues. Sources include meats, whole milk, cheese, ice cream and eggs. It is not necessary to eliminate these products from your diet, but it may be wise to reduce the total amount you eat. It is especially important to restrict these foods in the diets of families who have histories of cardiovascular disease.

Many high-fat foods are also high-sodium foods. When you begin to reduce one category, the other is also affected in a positive way.

Examples of How to Reduce Fat *and* Sodium

	Total Calories	Fat Calories	Sodium Mg.
1 oz. bologna	88	74	364
1 oz. lean roast beef	60	21	14
2 frankfurters (2 oz.)	220	162	928
2 oz. lean ground beef	94	21	28
3 oz. cured ham	300	216	616
3 oz. lean pork roast	205	79	73

Five Easy Ways To Reduce The Use Of Fat

(1) Use non-stick spray when frying or when a recipe calls for a buttered dish or pan.

(2) When you must sauté an ingredient, use a little vegetable broth in place of fat, or use a non-stick pan, or non-stick spray. Substitute a polyunsaturated oil for butter or margarine, and reduce the amount used.

(3) Whenever possible, reduce fats in dairy products called for in a recipe one step down, as follows:
Heavy Cream ⟶ Half and Half ⟶ Whole Milk ⟶ Lowfat Milk ⟶ Nonfat Milk

(4) Reduce the size of meat portions. Serve fish, poultry and dried bean dishes more often. Choose meat with less fat. Broil, bake, steam or barbecue instead of frying.

(5) Make your own sweets with polyunsaturated oils, nonfat milk and fewer eggs, and serve them less often. Rely more on fresh fruits for dessert.

You'll find these changes can be made without anyone feeling deprived. Food can even look and taste better without all the fat!

Here's how some of our favorite foods compare with each other in fat content:

FAT COMPARISON CHART
1 gram fat = 9 calories

FOODS	GRAMS FAT	FAT CALORIES
Tuna packed in water (½ cup)	.8	7.2
Chicken, light meat (3½ ozs.)	3.4	30.6
Creamed cottage cheese (3½ ozs.)	4.2	37.8
Chicken, dark meat (3½ ozs.)	5.7	50.0
Margarine (1 tbs.)	6.3	56.7
Fish, halibut, flounder, salmon (3 ozs.)	8.8	79.2
Cheddar cheese (1 oz.)	9.1	81.9
Cold cuts (2 slices)	9.5	85.5
Beef pot roast (½ lb. raw)	11.2	100.8
Bacon, broiled (3 strips)	13.5	121.5
Hamburger, regular (4 ozs.)	14.5	130.5
Rib-eye steak (1 small)	16.0	144.0

Turkey with Orange Glaze (page 121) ▶

Getting Started...

If you want to be well-nourished, but you DO NOT want to spend long hours in the kitchen, and if you **would** like to quiet the mid-afternoon worries about what to have for dinner, and the 5:30 stops at the supermarket, and you'd like to stop "throwing something together," then planning can be your indispensable aid! Take just thirty minutes to plan one weekly trip to the supermarket, and your life will be simplified immensely.

Planning pulls it all together: nutrition, a variety of foods, mouth-watering menus, use of leftovers, supermarket specials and the opportunity to try new recipes. Best of all, it saves time and releases you from much mental stress.

How do you do it? Once a week, gather together two sheets of paper, newspaper supermarket ads, your recipe file and calendar of activities. Mark one sheet of paper, "Grocery list"; mark the other, "Master Menu Plan". Divide the menu plan into seven columns, one for each day of the week.

You are ready to begin!

(1) Survey your refrigerator noting which foods need to be used quickly. Also note staples which must be replenished, and add these to your grocery list.

(2) After checking your calendar, note on your menu plan any outside activities that require an extra-quick meal, and any meals you are planning to eat away from home.

(3) Check the supermarket ads for food sales and produce in season.

(4) Now, armed with data, think through what you would like to prepare. Write the main dish first and then fill in with the other food choices. Consider:

nutritional balance	weekly specials	produce in season
color and texture	cooking times	your personal energy
variety	favorite recipes	"highs and lows"
food on hand		

(5) As you write, you can pull appropriate recipes, check your kitchen for needed ingredients and prepare your grocery list.

Voilà, a thirty-minute plan. With experience, you can reduce the time even further. You are now ready to shop for the week. (After shopping is a great time to prepare salad greens and raw vegetables for the week.)

Rest easy. No more worry about what to have for dinner. Because it is planned and on paper, you can do timely pre-preparations (pull the chicken out to thaw or mix up a marinade in the morning). Meal preparation proceeds smoothly. You know what's on the menu, the ingredients are on hand and the pre-preparation is complete. You are "in and out of the kitchen"—feeling confident that your family is well-fed, well-nourished and loved!

SAVING TIME WITH YOUR FREEZER

A freezer can be like an individualized grocery store. With today's busy schedules, it can be a great help in meal planning. Here are a few time-saving suggestions:

- Cook double portions and freeze the extras in containers that can be popped into a microwave or conventional oven.
- Leftovers can be frozen in microwave dinner trays or TV dinner trays. The frozen meals you prepare yourself will be more varied and more nutritious than those purchased at the supermarket.
- Freeze long-cooking items, such as spaghetti sauce, legumes and brown rice, in 1- or 2-cup containers ready to be used in many recipes.
- Purchase such foods as concentrated orange juice, frozen vegetables, bread, fish, meat and poultry on sale. Wrap well and store in your freezer.
- Muffins and slices of nut or fruit bread freeze well and can be placed in lunch pails while still frozen.
- Keep a jar in the freezer for collecting the broth from cooked vegetables until you have enough for a tasty soup. Save bits and pieces of leftover vegetables and meat for the soup, too.

- Freezers work more efficiently when full. Fill empty milk cartons with water to fill in empty freezer space. Use the ice-filled milk cartons in your food cooler when having a party or going picnicking.

Some helpful tips for better freezing:

- Use sturdy packaging and wrapping materials. Freezer containers should be airtight and moisture-proof. Choose heavy-duty aluminum foil, heavy-weight plastic wrap or bags, and made-for-freezer-plastic or glass containers.
- Cool cooked foods quickly before freezing.
- ALWAYS leave about one inch of space at the top of the container for the food to expand during freezing.
- Label each item with content and date.
- Move existing foods to the front, as new ones are added to the freezer, and use them first.
- Do not re-freeze. Re-freezing decreases the quality of the food and reduces nutrition.

Average storage time for cooked foods that are properly packaged:

Muffins: 2 to 3 months

Yeast breads: 6 months

Seafood, meat, poultry: 3 to 4 months

Mixed dishes, pasta, stews: 3 months

OTHER TIME-SAVING EQUIPMENT

Modern, time-saving appliances are a boon to busy folks who cook! Lucky for our budgets, many of these once-expensive items are now priced within the reach of most of us.

Here are our choices of appliances that we feel are most helpful to the busy cook:

MICROWAVE OVEN

This modern marvel defrosts foods quickly, reheats leftovers while preserving taste and appearance, and cooks so speedily that you may find yourself reintroducing foods to your family that take too long to cook conventionally. Baked potatoes, for example, can be served much more often when they cook in minutes (4 minutes for one; 8 minutes for two) instead of an hour or more.

An important advantage to microwave cooking is that it preserves nutrients that are lost in longer cooking.

Easy clean-up is appreciated by busy people. You can cook and serve on the same plate. No more messy pots and pans to discourage you from full-meal preparation.

And, last, but not least, microwave ovens are energy-efficient.

A note of caution: Not all foods cook as well in a microwave oven as they do by conventional methods. Often, the time saved is more important than the quality lost. Each cook has to judge this for himself or herself.

If you cook most of your food in a microwave oven, you may need to reorganize your meal-preparation plan. Foods that maintain heat longest should be cooked first.

Microwave ovens also require certain types of special dishes and you may want to invest in a few basic ones. A class in microwave cooking is extremely helpful in making these decisions, and in getting you off to a good start. If taking a class is impossible, follow the directions as outlined in the cookbook delivered with the oven.

FOOD PROCESSOR

"Lickity-split" is the way this handy appliance does its job. When you're in a hurry and there's chopping and mixing to be done, a food processor is your greatest assistant. It is excellent for time-consuming chores such as chopping nuts, making bread crumbs, and grating cheese.

Look at every recipe with the food processor in mind. No need to wash the bowl after each use. Chop dry ingredients first, then wet (nuts or crumbs before apples or onions). Also, strong foods such as onions should be the last processed, unless you're mixing meat loaf and it doesn't matter.

Be sure to use a light "on and off" touch to avoid over-processing.

BLENDER

A blender will do many jobs. It can whip-up smooth cottage cheese dressings and dips, blend ingredients, puree cooked vegetables and mix beverages like nothing else can. It is easy to use and takes little space.

It is not necessary to purchase one with a large number of settings. "Low," "Medium" and "High" will do everything you need to do. One with a removable blade for easier cleaning is the best choice.

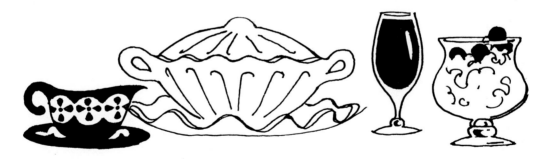

Appetizers and Snacks

The recipes in this section were chosen for their appeal to both adults and children. Children need snacks for extra nutrition and energy. Too often children's snacks are high in fat and salt and are nutrient-poor.

In addition to the recipes in this section, consider these easy snack ideas:

1. Keep a transparent refrigerator jar filled with colorful and crunchy carrot sticks, cucumber slices and zucchini stalks.
2. Fill celery with peanut butter or cream cheese and cut into bite-size pieces.
3. Keep a bowl of colorful, ready-to-eat fresh fruit handy.
4. Top whole wheat or rye crackers with mozzarella cheese, peanut butter or garbanzo spread.
5. Keep a variety of muffins in the freezer. Pop in the microwave for 25 seconds or let stand at room temperature for half an hour.
6. Make your own fruit pops by diluting fruit juices 1 part juice to 1 part water. Freeze in ice cube trays or pour into small paper cups; cover with foil. Make a slit in center of cover and insert popsicle stick.

7. Make quesadillas by placing a flour tortilla in an ironstone skillet over moderate heat. Cover one half of the tortilla with grated cheese; fold the other half over cheese. Pan broil on both sides until the cheese melts; cut into 4 wedges.

Most of the following recipes can double as appetizers for adult parties. Many people appreciate finding low-calorie edibles on a party table.

Crunchy, Cheesy Snacks

Tempt children and adults to snack on raw vegetables by stuffing them with this cheese mixture. The dairy products provide calcium and protein, while the vegetables provide crunch and fiber.

2 cups (8 ozs.) cheddar cheese
8 ozs. cream cheese, softened
¼ cup plain low-fat yogurt
celery, green pepper wedges, cucumber chunks, zucchini slices, cherry tomatoes

Grate cheddar cheese in food processor. Add cream cheese and yogurt. Process until smooth. Add more yogurt if mixture is too stiff. Stuff or spread vegetables with cheese mixture, or use as spread for bread or crackers.

Variations

Add 1 tablespoon minced green onions to cheese mixture.
Add ½ cup finely chopped walnuts to cheese mixture.
Add ½ cup unsalted sunflower seeds to cheese mixture.

"Yes, You Can" Dips

Dips can be nutritious and taste good without anyone realizing that they aren't loaded with fat calories. Try these for starters, then add your own imaginative variations. Chill for several hours to allow flavors to develop and blend.

Herb Dip
Makes: 1 cup

1 cup plain low-fat yogurt
1 tsp. grated onion
1 tsp. chopped green onion
½ tsp. caraway seeds
¼ tsp. summer savory

Combine ingredients and chill.

Curry Dip
Makes: 1 cup

1 cup plain low-fat yogurt
3 tbs. mayonnaise
2 to 3 tsp. curry powder
salt to taste

Combine ingredients and chill.

Tuna Dip
Makes: 2 cups

1 cup plain low-fat yogurt
½ cup water-packed tuna
½ cup finely chopped cucumber
1 tbs. lemon juice
2 tsp. minced green onion

Combine ingredients and chill.

"Sour Cream"
Makes: 1 cup

1 cup low-fat cottage cheese
2 tbs. nonfat milk
1 tbs. lemon juice

Combine ingredients in a blender container and blend on high speed until smooth. Chill. Use as topping for baked potatoes or in dips.

Variations

Herb Dip: Add 1 teaspoon minced onion and ½ teaspoon caraway seeds to "Sour Cream." Chill.

Poppy Seed Dip: Add 1 teaspoon **each** honey and poppy seeds, and ½ teaspoon cinnamon to "Sour Cream." Chill. This is good with fruit such as apples and pears.

Dilly Dip: Add 3 tablespoons minced dill pickle and 1 tablespoon minced green onion to "Sour Cream." Chill.

Spectacular Platter

Colorful for a party buffet as the salad or vegetable course for a light summer meal. Keep marinated vegetables on hand for a healthy snack.

1 small stalk broccoli
1 cup small button mushrooms
½ head cauliflower, broken into
   floweretes
¼ pound green beans
½ cup carrot sticks
1 cup cooked garbanzo **or**
   kidney beans, drained

Zesty Herb Dressing, page 78
½ zucchini, thinly sliced
½ green pepper, sliced into rings
1 tomato, cut in wedges
1 small red onion, thinly sliced
1 pound mozzarella cheese, cut in cubes
¼ cup chopped fresh parsley

Separate broccoli flowerets from stems. Peel stems and slice. Steam mushrooms, broccoli, cauliflower, green beans and carrot sticks until crisp-tender. Marinate steamed vegetables and garbanzos in vinaigrette dressing overnight. Drain vegetables and save marinade. Arrange marinated vegetables in the center of a large platter. Garnish with zucchini slices, green pepper rings, tomato wedges, onion rings and cheese. Drizzle marinade over entire platter. Sprinkle parsley over all.

Mushrooms Parmesan *Great!*

A quick, easy and nutritious appetizer that avoids the high-fat mixtures often found in stuffed mushrooms. Prepare ahead and refrigerate. (Be sure to increase microwave time approximately 30 seconds.)

2 dozen large mushrooms (2 inches in diameter)
1 tbs. margarine
4 green onions, finely chopped
dash garlic powder
½ cup Parmesan cheese

Wash mushrooms and drain well on paper towels. Remove stems and chop. Melt margarine in bowl in microwave oven. Add stems, green onions and garlic powder. Microwave 2 minutes. (Or sauté in fry pan until soft.) Add Parmesan cheese to mixture. Fill mushroom caps. Microwave 2 to 3 minutes until soft, or bake in 400°F. oven for 10 to 12 minutes.

Cereal Combo

Watch this one disappear! A lower-salt, lower-fat alternative to cereal-nut snack blends.

1 cup Wheat Chex
1 cup Corn Chex
1 cup Rice Chex
1 cup pretzel sticks **or**
  chow mein noodles
1 cup roasted unsalted pumpkin seeds

1 cup roasted unsalted peanuts
½ cup walnuts
6 tbs. margarine
4 tsp. Worcestershire sauce
1 tsp. garlic powder **or** onion powder
½ cup raisins (optional)

Mix cereals, pretzel sticks, seeds and nuts together in a large bowl. Melt margarine. Stir in Worcestershire sauce and garlic powder. Pour over cereal mixture and toss until blended. Spread mixture into a shallow pan. Bake 40 minutes in 275°F. oven. Stir several times. Cool and store in airtight container. Add raisins just before serving.

Microwave: Mix cereals, pretzel sticks, seeds and nuts together in shallow microwave-safe dish. Microwave margarine and seasonings approximately 45 seconds. Pour over cereal-nut mixture and toss until well mixed. Microwave, uncovered, approximately 8 minutes, stirring occasionally. Store in airtight container. Add raisins just before serving.

Nachos

These disappear in a hurry, but it's easy to make more!

Cut corn tortillas in eighths and layer on a paper or plastic plate for microwave; glass or metal for oven. Add shredded Mozzarella or Jack cheese (Jack has more flavor, but is higher in fat). Top with chopped green chilies and onions. Microwave uncovered 45 to 60 seconds. Or broil in oven until cheese melts and is bubbly. Add chopped tomatoes for garnish.

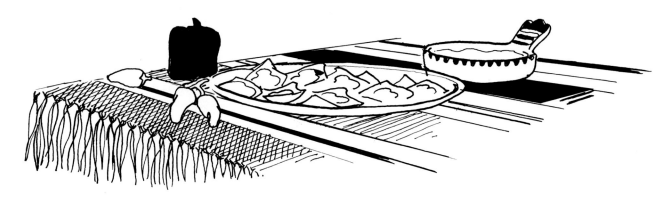

Preparation time: 5 minutes
Servings: 1

Grape Fizz

A special summer refresher for children and adults—so good it often substitutes for dessert. For each serving:

1 tall glass
½ cup grape juice
1 scoop vanilla ice milk
club soda to fill glass

Add ingredients to glass in order listed. Garnish with a sprig of mint. Serve with a straw and an iced tea spoon.

Preparation time: 20 to 25
minutes
Baking time: 15 to 18 minutes
Makes: 33

Cheese Pretzels

A fun treat for children and adults. Easy to make, quick to bake.

1 tbs. active dry yeast
1½ cups warm water
1 tsp. salt
1 tbs. sugar
3½ cups flour
1 cup grated cheddar cheese
1 egg, beaten

Dissolve yeast, salt and sugar in water in food processor bowl. Add 3½ cups flour and cheese. Mix by turning processor "on-off" a few times. Then run about one minute to knead dough until smooth. (If dough sticks, add more flour.) Form a roll. Cut into 33 pieces. Roll each piece into a rope 14 inches long. Twist into pretzel shape. Place on ungreased baking sheet. Brush with beaten egg. Bake 15 to 18 minutes in 425°F. oven.

Lentil Soup (page 70) ▶

Soups

Homemade soups are a natural for good nutrition. Everything we have been talking about comes together in a bowl of soup. Vitamins, minerals and fiber are in abundance because you use fresh vegetables, leftover vegetable cooking water and whole grains. Soups are low in fat if you skim the fat off the broth after it has cooled. By using herbs and spices you can keep salt to a minimum. Be creative, use your leftovers and enjoy a bowl of soup as an appetizer or as the main dish. Make a double recipe of soup and freeze the extra for later use.

Preparation time: 10 minutes
Cooking time: 2 hours
Makes: 12 cups

Basic Chicken Broth

Chicken broth is the basis of many soups, and an important ingredient in many recipes. It can be purchased in cans, but it is easy and more economical to make it yourself. Make it from the bony pieces, such as necks, backs and wings, which you can collect and freeze until you have enough, or use chicken pieces or a whole chicken. A turkey carcass or turkey parts make good broth, too. Freeze the broth in pint or quart containers or in ice cube trays. The cubes are handy for recipes calling for small amounts of broth. For a quick meal soup, add noodles or rice, frozen vegetables and pieces of cooked chicken to prepared broth.

3 to 4 lbs. chicken **or** turkey parts
1 large onion, chopped
1 stalk celery with leaves, sliced
1 bay leaf

2 cloves garlic, peeled and minced
8 peppercorns
3 qts. water

Place chicken in large pot. Add remaining ingredients. Bring to a boil. Reduce heat, cover and simmer about 2 hours. Remove chicken from bones and use to make salad or a casserole dish. Strain broth and chill. Remove hardened fat. Freeze broth if not using right away.

Preparation time: 15 minutes
Chilling time: 4 hours
Servings: 8

Gazpacho

Here's a refreshing way to eat your vegetables on a warm day. Put your processor to work and it's done in minutes.

½ cup diced, peeled and seeded cucumber
4 ripe tomatoes, peeled, seeded and finely chopped
⅓ cup finely chopped onion
½ cup finely chopped green pepper
¼ cup olive oil
¼ cup cider or wine vinegar
2 cups tomato juice
¼ tsp. black pepper
1 clove garlic, finely chopped (optional)

Combine all ingredients in large mixing bowl. Cover and chill at least 4 hours. Serve in chilled bowls or cups.

Preparation time: 8 to 10 minutes
Cooking time: 8 to 10 minutes
Servings: 6

Broccoli Bisque Good

Serve this delicious soup hot or icy cold, garnished with lemon slices. It is packed with good nutrition and can be made in a hurry. Omit curry, if desired.

2 tbs. margarine
1¼ to 1½ pounds fresh broccoli, trimmed and chopped
1 medium onion, coarsely chopped
½ to 1 tsp. curry powder
½ tsp. salt
dash freshly ground pepper
3½ cups chicken broth
2 tbs. lime juice

Melt margarine in large saucepan over medium heat. Add broccoli, onion and curry powder. Sauté a minute or two, but do not allow onion to brown. Add salt, pepper and broth. Stir until mixed. Cover and bring to boil. Reduce heat and simmer until broccoli is just tender, about 8 to 10 minutes. Cool slightly, then pour half of mixture into blender container. Cover and blend until smooth. Repeat with remaining mixture. Add lime juice. Reheat and serve, or chill at least 4 hours. Garnish with lemon slices.

Preparation time: 10 minutes
Cooking time: 14 minutes
Servings: 4

Quick Potato Soup

"Cream" soups are a good source of calcium and protein. It's an easy way to get all the nutrients of milk, plus vegetables. Use nonfat milk and the soup will be low in fat.

3 cups water **or** chicken broth
2 cups diced, raw potatoes
½ cup finely chopped onion
½ tsp. salt (optional)
1 cup instant nonfat dry milk
2 tbs. margarine
pepper to taste
parsley, dill weed or nutmeg

Measure 2 cups water into a 2½ quart bowl. Cover and microwave on High 4 minutes. Add potatoes, onions and salt. Cover and microwave 12 minutes until potatoes are tender (time will vary with variety of potatoes used). Combine instant milk with remaining 1 cup water. Stir until dissolved. Add milk, margarine and pepper to potatoes. Microwave 2 minutes. Stir and serve. Garnish with parsley, dill weed or nutmeg.

Preparation time: 10 minutes
Cooking time: 2 hours
Servings: 6

Split Pea Soup

A thick, robust soup that provides protein. Use your food processor to chop the vegetables. Serve for lunch or a light dinner.

2 cups split peas
6 cups water
1 cup chopped onion
2 carrots, chopped
2 stalks celery, chopped
2 cloves garlic, minced

2 tsp. brown mustard
½ tsp. **each** marjoram, thyme
   and salt (optional)
pepper to taste
½ cup Vermouth **or** Sherry
plain yogurt

Combine peas and water in large pot. Bring to boil. Reduce heat and simmer 2 hours. Add vegetables, mustard, herbs, salt and pepper. Cook 30 minutes. Add Vermouth and heat. Serve in warm bowls. Top each bowl with a dollop of yogurt.

Preparation time: 10 minutes
Cooking time: 2 hours
Servings: 4 to 6

Lentil Soup

A good source of protein. Serve at lunch or for dinner with salad and crusty bread.

2 cups lentils
6 cups water
½ tsp. pepper
1 cup chopped onion
1 clove garlic, minced
1 bay leaf
2 whole cloves
6 slices fresh lemon (optional)

Rinse lentils; drain and place in large pot with water. Add remaining ingredients. Cover and simmer 2 hours. Remove bay leaf. Garnish each bowl with a lemon slice.

Preparation time: 20 minutes
Cooking time: 2½ hours
Servings: 6

Babci's Chicken Soup

My best friend gave me her grandmother's tasty soup recipe. Serve with crusty bread, cheese and fruit.

1 chicken, 3 to 4 lbs.
water
1 onion, sliced
1 cinnamon stick
4 **each** whole cloves and
   whole allspice

1 tsp. chopped parsley
½ head cabbage, cut in small wedges
1 carrot, sliced thin
½ tsp. dill weed
½ tsp. salt (optional)
2 raw potatoes cut in small pieces

Place chicken in large pot. Add water to cover, onion, cinnamon, cloves and allspice. Bring to boil, reduce heat and simmer uncovered 1½ to 2 hours. Strain broth and remove chicken from bones. Cut into small pieces and refrigerate. Skim fat (this is easier if you chill the stock overnight). Add remaining ingredients to degreased broth and cook 45 minutes. Add chicken and cook 15 minutes. Serve in heated bowls.

Preparation time: 10 minutes
Cooking time: 30 minutes
Servings: 4 to 6

Tuna Vegetable Soup

Enjoy a complete meal with fresh vegetables and tuna that is flavorful but low in sodium.

6 cups chicken broth
1 bunch broccoli, chopped
3 carrots, sliced
½ tsp. thyme
½ tsp. Tabasco sauce
1 can (7 ozs.) tuna, packed in water

Bring stock to boil in a large pot. Reduce heat. Add vegetables and seasonings. Simmer 30 minutes or until vegetables are tender. Drain tuna and add just before serving.

Preparation time: 20 minutes
Cooking time: 30 minutes
Servings: 4 to 6

Minestrone *Great!*

This hearty vegetable soup can be varied by changing the vegetables and type of pasta. Have a complete meal by adding tossed salad, French bread and fruit for dessert.

1 cup chopped onion
2 garlic cloves, minced
2 tbs. vegetable oil
¼ tsp. pepper
1 tsp. dried oregano
1 tsp. dried basil
1 cup diced carrots
1 cup sliced celery

1 cup sliced zucchini
4 cups chicken **or** turkey broth
One can (16 ozs.) tomato puree
1 cup cooked navy **or** garbanzo beans
¼ cup red wine
1 cup tomatoes, chopped
¾ cup uncooked elbow macaroni

Sauté onion and garlic in vegetable oil in large pot. Add remaining ingredients and bring to a boil. Reduce heat, cover and simmer for 30 minutes.

Salads

Americans love salads! Almost every dinner menu includes one. It is a standard accompaniment to restaurant dining. Even fast food restaurants offer salad bars.

This love affair with salads doesn't always continue into the home. Clients tell us that it takes too much time to prepare a salad every evening.

The key is pre-preparation. Make it a simple, once-a-week project. Right after shopping, when everything is at its freshest, is a good time to get organized. Wash greens and non-juicy vegetables (radishes, green peppers, green onions, carrots, red cabbage) under cold, running water. Shake off excess water and then thoroughly dry in a lettuce spinner, or place greens in a clean pillowcase, reserved for just this purpose. Either take the case outside and swing it around until centrifugal force displaces the water, or place it in your automatic washer on "spin dry." Store dried greens in an airtight container in the refrigerator. Voilà! Instant salad. Added ingredients can change with each meal.

Salads can be the main course and/or contribute to any part of the meal—as the protein dish (Peachy Chicken Salad, page 86) the starch dish (Confetti Rice Salad, page 83) the vegetable (Corn and Lima Salad, page 83).

The recipes in this section were chosen for their eye appeal, nutrition and roughage.

◀ **Spicy Yogurt Dressing (page 79)**
Tossed Green Salad (page 76)

Tossed Green Salads

The success of a salad depends on crisp greens. Wash greens well under cold, running water. Drain and thoroughly dry in a salad spinner or on paper towels. Store in an airtight container in the refrigerator. Vary each salad by using a variety of ingredients as suggested below. Begin with crisp greens, add other ingredients, as desired, and your choice of dressing. See Zesty Herb Dressing (page 78) and Spicy Yogurt Dressing (page 79).

Crisp greens—lettuce, spinach, chard, endive, escarole, watercress or parsley
  or a combination

Low-Cal Additions:

Alfalfa sprouts	Celery	Raw turnips
Bean sprouts	Cucumbers	Rutabaga
Beets	Green beans	Summer squash
Broccoli flowers and/or stems	Onions	Tomatoes
Carrots	Radishes	Zucchini slices
Cauliflower		

For a main-dish salad, add any of the following, **plus** other additions of your choice.

Cheese
Chicken
Dried beans—garbanzo, kidney, pinto, etc.
Lean meat

Nuts
Seeds
Tuna or other flaked fish
Turkey

Preparation time: 5 minutes
Makes: 1 cup

Zesty Herb Dressing

¼ cup lemon juice
¼ cup wine vinegar
½ cup poly-unsaturated oil
2 tsp. minced onion
½ tsp. **each** basil, sugar, paprika and mustard
⅛ tsp. ground pepper

Beat all ingredients together with wire whip. Chill.

Variations:

Add 1 tablespoon catsup and ½ to 1 teaspoon Worcestershire sauce.
Omit onion and basil for a simple oil and vinegar dressing.

Preparation time: 5 minutes
Makes: 1¼ cups

Spicy Yogurt Dressing

½ cup plain yogurt
½ cup nonfat milk
¼ cup lemon juice
¼ tsp. **each** dill weed, dry mustard, garlic powder, salt
⅛ tsp. **each** thyme and sugar

Blend all ingredients with wire whip. Chill.

Preparation time: 25 minutes
Servings: 6 to 8

Marinated Raw Vegetable Salad

This assortment of marinated raw vegetables makes an "instant" salad.

8 cups assorted fresh vegetables: zucchini sticks, carrot sticks,
    mushroom slices, cucumber slices, cherry tomatoes, and
    broccoli flowerets
¾ cup lemon juice
¾ cup vegetable oil
2 tbs. sugar
1½ tsp. oregano
½ tsp. pepper
½ tsp. dill weed
½ tsp. salt

Place vegetables in a shallow glass dish. Combine remaining ingredients in a 4-cup measure. Pour over vegetables. Refrigerate for several hours. Stir occasionally. Serve in lettuce cups.

Stir-Fried Chicken (page 120) ▶

Corn and Lima Salad

This colorful patio dish can take the place of potatoes, rice or other starch in your meal planning. Try it with grilled pork steaks, apple compote and French bread.

1 pkg. (10 ozs.) frozen lima beans
1 can (12 ozs.) whole kernel corn, drained
¼ cup mayonnaise
¼ cup sweet pickle relish
1 tsp. cider vinegar

Cook limas early in day. Drain and combine with corn. Chill. Ten minutes before serving, add remaining ingredients. Toss lightly. Serve in salad bowl lined with lettuce leaves. Excellent the second day.

Confetti Rice Salad

A colorful and crunchy summer salad or buffet dish.

1½ cups cooked brown rice, chilled
1 tomato, diced
¼ green pepper, diced
¼ red pepper, diced **or** 1 whole pimiento, chopped
1 onion, minced (Bermuda if available)
1½ tsp. chopped fresh parsley
4 tbs. Zesty Herb Dressing, page 78
¼ tsp. curry
1 tbs. raisins

Place rice in large mixing bowl. Add vegetables, dressing, curry and raisins. Toss lightly.

Tabbouli

This salad is a favorite in the Middle Eastern countries. It is perfect for a patio party because it goes well with a variety of other foods and can be made ahead.

1 cup uncooked bulgur
2 cups boiling water
2 tomatoes, finely diced
1 bunch green onions with tops, finely chopped
1 cup finely chopped parsley
3 tbs. chopped fresh mint **or** 2 tsp. dry mint flakes
¼ cup vegetable oil
¼ cup lemon juice
½ tsp. salt
¼ tsp. cumin
freshly ground pepper, to taste

Place bulgur in mixing bowl. Pour boiling water over it. Allow to stand 1 hour. Drain well, then squeeze out as much moisture as possible. Add remaining ingredients and mix well. Chill. Serve on a bed of lettuce.

Quick and Light Potato Salad

A colorful and crunchy potato salad, lighter in calories and salt. Serve with slices of cold meat or poultry for a summertime meal. To save time, cook the potatoes in microwave oven and chop the vegetables in food processor.

2 cups diced cooked potatoes
¼ cup **each** chopped celery, green pepper, radishes and cucumber
¼ cup finely chopped onion
⅓ cup low-calorie mayonnaise
⅓ cup plain low-fat yogurt
1 tbs. vinegar
2 to 3 tsp. mustard
½ tsp. sugar
½ tsp. celery seed

Toss potatoes and chopped vegetables together in mixing bowl. Make dressing of mayonnaise, yogurt, vinegar, mustard, sugar and celery seed. Toss with potato mixture. Chill. Serve in lettuce cups.

Peachy Chicken Salad

A colorful, crunchy salad that looks pretty, tastes good and offers nutrition plus. For a cool, light, summer supper or a refreshing luncheon, serve with soup, muffins and a light dessert.

1 cup cooked brown rice
2 cups diced cooked chicken
½ cup **each** celery and green pepper, coarsely chopped
1½ cups cubed fresh **or** canned peaches, drained
¼ cup chopped walnuts **or** almonds
¼ cup mayonnaise
1 tbs. chopped onion
1½ tsp. curry powder
1 tbs. lemon juice

Lightly toss together the rice, chicken, celery, green pepper, peaches and nuts. Make dressing of mayonnaise, onion, curry and lemon juice. Stir dressing into mixture. Chill thoroughly. Serve in lettuce cups. Garnish with toasted walnuts or almonds.

Peachy Chicken Salad (page 86) ▶

Vegetables

Vegetables are an extremely important part of our daily meal plan as they provide vitamins and minerals that might otherwise be forgotten. They add color, flavor and texture to our meals. Choose fresh vegetables, store properly and cook just until crisp-tender.

VEGETABLE GUIDELINES

- Store root vegetables in a cool, dry area. Do not store potatoes and onions near each other.
- Store delicate vegetables in the refrigerator in tightly closed containers or plastic bags.
- Always wash vegetables well, but do not soak in water because water soluble nutrients will be lost.
- Cook vegetables with skins on whenever possible. Valuable vitamins are stored just beneath the skin and are lost with the peelings.
- Microwave, steam, bake or boil vegetables in as little water as possible to retain water-soluble vitamins. Steaming and microwaving preserve the most nutrients.

- **To Steam:** Use a collapsible steaming basket which adjusts to various size pans. Be sure the pan used has a tight-fitting lid to prevent steam from escaping. Do not allow the water to come above the bottom of the basket.
- **To Microwave:** Arrange vegetables in a microwave-safe dish. Add about ¼ cup of water. Cover tightly with lid or plastic wrap. Microwave on High until fork tender. Check your instruction booklet for exact directions.
- **To Boil:** Use only enough liquid to prevent vegetables from sticking to pan. Keep pot tightly covered and cook as quickly as possible. Watch carefully to prevent overcooking.
- **To Bake:** Vegetables such as potatoes, winter squash and tomatoes bake right in their skins. Mushrooms, summer squash and carrots can be baked in a covered casserole dish with a small amount of liquid added. Bake in a 350°F. oven until fork tender.
- **To Stir-Fry:** Quickly sauté vegetables in a small amount of oil in a large frying pan or wok over high heat. Stir and gently toss vegetables as they cook. Cook only until crisp tender.

THERE'S MORE THAN ONE WAY
TO SEASON A VEGETABLE!

Herbs and spices add zest to potatoes and other vegetables. You will find you need less margarine and salt won't be missed.

Herbs and Vegetables That Go Well Together

 THYME
Beets
Onions
Carrots
Green Beans

 BASIL
Onions
Eggplant
Squash
Tomatoes
Beets

 BAY LEAF
Stewed Tomatoes
Add to water when cooking
   Potatoes
   Carrots

 MARJORAM
Mushrooms
Zucchini
Peas
Spinach
Green Beans

 OREGANO
Tomatoes
Cabbage
Lentils
Broccoli

 DILL WEED
Green Beans
Cucumbers
New Potatoes
Asparagus

 MINT
Carrots
New Potatoes
Spinach
Peas

 ROSEMARY
Mushrooms
Peas
Spinach
Squash

 SAGE
Onions
Tomatoes
Eggplant
Lima Beans

 SAVORY
Mushrooms
Peas
Green Beans
Beets

Use herbs sparingly…to bring out and enhance the natural flavor of the vegetable, not to overpower it.

Glorified Margarine

Add desired seasonings to melted margarine. Allow to stand to develop flavor. Serve over hot vegetables or baked potatoes.

Melt ¼ cup margarine.

For:	Add:
Lemon Margarine	— 2 tbs. lemon juice, ¼ tsp. grated lemon peel, dash pepper
Herb Margarine	— 1 tsp. parsley, ¼ tsp. oregano, thyme, marjoram, basil **or** rosemary
Italian Margarine	— 1 tsp. lemon juice, ½ tsp. basil, ¼ tsp. oregano
Parmesan Margarine	— 1 tbs. Parmesan cheese, ¾ tsp. basil, ¾ tsp. marjoram
Curried Margarine	— 2 tbs. lemon juice, ¼ tsp. curry powder, dash pepper
Onion Margarine	— 1 tsp. grated onion, 1 tbs. minced parsley
Celery Margarine	— 1 tsp. celery seeds
Garlic Margarine	— 1 small clove garlic, peeled and cut in half (remove before serving)
Mustard Margarine	— ¼ tsp. dried or prepared mustard, 1 tsp. lemon juice, dash sugar
Nut Margarine	— ¼ cup nuts—sauté until golden, add 2 tsp. lemon juice

Today's "Cream" Sauce

Sauces are an easy way to dress up vegetables. In fact, a "cream" sauce can be combined with vegetables, meat, hard-cooked eggs or fish and served over toast, pasta or rice for a quick nutritious meal.

1 tbs. margarine
1 tbs. flour
⅛ tsp. white pepper
1 cup lowfat **or** nonfat milk

Microwave: Place margarine in a 2-cup glass measure. Microwave on Medium until melted. Blend in flour, pepper and milk. Microwave on High 2 minutes. Stir and continue cooking on High for 1 to 1½ minutes or until thickened.

Conventional: Melt margarine in a saucepan over medium heat. Blend in flour and pepper. Cook, stirring, 1 minute. Remove from heat and stir in milk. Return to heat and cook, stirring constantly, until sauce thickens and boils.

Variations:

- Sauté ½ cup sliced fresh mushrooms in margarine before adding flour.
- Sauté ¼ cup chopped onion in margarine before adding flour.
- Add 1 cup shredded cheese and ¼ teaspoon dry mustard to thickened sauce. Stir until cheese melts, or microwave 1 minute.
- Add 1 teaspoon freshly chopped herbs, such as parsley or dill, to thickened sauce.
- Add ½ teaspoon dried herbs, such as thyme or oregano, to thickened sauce.
- Stir 2 teaspoons curry powder and ¼ teaspoon ground ginger into melted margarine before adding flour.
- Add prepared mustard and lemon juice, to taste, to thickened sauce.
- Fold 2 diced hard-cooked eggs into thickened sauce.

Broccoli with Lemon Sauce

1 bunch fresh broccoli
¼ cup water
2 tbs. margarine
1 tbs. flour

½ cup skim **or** low-fat milk
1 tsp. grated lemon peel
1 tbs. lemon juice
¼ tsp. ground ginger

Microwave: Wash broccoli and remove large leaves and tough parts of stalks. Separate and cut into individual spears. Arrange in shallow 1½ quart baking dish with stalks toward outside. Add water and microwave 6 to 8 minutes on High. Set aside. In small bowl, microwave margarine on High 30 seconds. Stir in flour until smooth. Gradually stir in milk. Microwave, uncovered, 2 to 3 minutes on High or until thickened and smooth. Stir in lemon peel, juice and ginger until well blended. Spoon sauce over broccoli. Heat 2 to 3 minutes on Roast or until thoroughly heated.

Conventional: Steam broccoli stalks until tender. While broccoli is cooking, melt margarine in a small pan over medium heat. Stir in flour until smooth. Gradually stir in milk. Cook, stirring constantly, until thickened. Stir in lemon peel, juice and ginger. Arrange broccoli in serving dish and spoon sauce over top.

Trout Almondine (page 107) ▶
Orange Carrots (page 96)

Orange Carrots

Great source of vitamin A.

½ cup water
2½ cups sliced carrots
½ cup orange juice
1 tbs. cornstarch
2 tbs. margarine
1 large orange, sectioned

Microwave: Combine carrots and water in a microwave-safe baking dish. Microwave on High for 6 to 7 minutes. Drain liquid into 4-cup measure. Add orange juice and cornstarch. Stir until blended. Microwave on Medium until thickened and clear. Add margarine and orange sections. Heat thoroughly and pour over cooked carrots.

Conventional: Bring water to boil. Add carrots, cover and cook until tender. Drain liquid into measuring cup. Set carrots aside. Add orange juice to carrot liquid to make 1 cup. Combine with cornstarch. Cook over medium heat until thickened and clear. Add margarine, carrots and orange sections. Heat thoroughly.

Stir-Fry Vegetable Medley

Simple, stir-fried vegetables enhance any meal. Prepare and cook the vegetables at the last moment to retain all the vitamins and minerals. This combination is a good source of vitamins A and C and fiber.

1 tbs. vegetable oil
2 carrots, sliced diagonally
2 zucchini, cut in strips
1 cup sliced mushrooms
1 large sweet pepper, thinly sliced

Heat oil in large skillet or wok. Add carrots and cook 2 to 3 minutes, stirring constantly. Add zucchini, mushrooms and pepper. Continue to stir-fry 3 to 4 minutes longer until vegetables are tender, yet crisp.

Preparation time: 15 minutes
Servings: 6

Ratatouille In a Hurry

This traditional vegetable dish may be served hot or cold.

¼ cup vegetable oil
1 cup thinly sliced onion
1 clove garlic, crushed
1 pound zucchini, thinly sliced
1 eggplant, cut in ½-inch cubes
1 green pepper, thinly sliced

3 large ripe tomatoes, cut into wedges
1 cup sliced mushrooms
2 tsp. basil
2 tsp. marjoram
½ tsp. pepper
½ tsp. salt

In a 3-quart, heat-resistant casserole dish, microwave oil, onions and garlic on High 5 minutes or until onions and garlic are tender. Add eggplant, zucchini and green pepper. Microwave, covered, on High 5 minutes. Add remaining ingredients and stir well. Microwave, uncovered, on High 5 minutes or until vegetables are tender.

Baked Potatoes

Garnish your potatoes with imagination. Try our "Sour Cream," page 55, or plain yogurt, and top with chopped chives, green onions, green peppers, or a sprinkling of dill weed.

Microwave: Pick uniform potatoes of medium size, (6 to 8 ounces). If potatoes are larger, they will take more time. Scrub potatoes well and prick several times with a fork. On a paper towel or plate, arrange potatoes in a circle with none in the center, and one inch of space between each potato. Microwave on High as follows:

1 potato	3½ to 4 minutes	4 potatoes	10 to 11 minutes
2 potatoes	6½ to 7 minutes	5 potatoes	13 to 14 minutes
3 potatoes	8½ to 9 minutes	6 potatoes	15 to 16 minutes

Potatoes continue to cook after they are removed from the oven, so don't overcook.

Conventional: Select uniform baking potatoes. Scrub well and prick several times with a fork. Bake in 425°F. oven 40 to 60 minutes. Cut a criss-cross in top of potato. Press ends, push up and fluff potato. Serve immediately.

Fish

Fish is a good source of protein, high in B vitamins, thiamin, riboflavin, niacin and many minerals. It is low in calories, high in polyunsaturated fats and delicious for any meal. Buy fish fresh whenever possible. If buying a whole fish, look for firm flesh, shiny scales and bright protruding eyes. Thaw frozen fish in the refrigerator and do not refreeze. To enhance the flavor of fish, season lightly with lemon juice or a favorite herb. Be careful not to over cook it and serve immediately.

Poached Fish

No fat calories here!

2½ lbs. fish fillets
¼ cup finely chopped onion
1 cup dry white wine **or** tomato juice **or** clam juice
lemon slices

Microwave: Lightly oil a shallow, microwave-safe baking dish. Place fillets in dish. Sprinkle with onions and pour wine over fish. Cover tightly. Microwave on High 10 minutes until fish flakes.

Conventional: In a large skillet heat wine to boiling. Reduce heat. Add fish and onion. Simmer 8 to 10 minutes. Remove with slotted spoon. Garnish with lemon.

Microwave's Marvelous Fish

This is a perfect recipe for cooking any kind of fish fillet.

1 lb. fish fillets
3 tbs. margarine
1 tbs. chopped fresh parsley
2 tbs. fresh lemon juice
dash pepper

Thaw fish if frozen. Measure margarine into a microwave-safe dish big enough to hold the fish in a single layer. Microwave at 50% power for 2 minutes or until melted. Blend 1 tablespoon of the parsley with melted margarine. Dip each fillet in the parsley-butter sauce, coating both sides. Arrange fillets with thick sides toward the outside of the dish. Pour lemon juice evenly over fillets. Sprinkle pepper and remaining 1 tablespoon parsley. Cover tightly with plastic wrap. Microwave at 100% power 6 to 8 minutes or until fish flakes easily with a fork. Let rest, covered, 4 minutes before serving.

Stuffed Fillets of Sole (page 106) ▶

Preparation time: 15 minutes
Servings: 4

Broiled Fish Steaks

This is a popular way to prepare fish. Children, particularly, like their fish broiled.

1½ lbs. fish steaks, about ¾-inch thick
¼ cup margarine
⅛ tsp. pepper
2 tbs. lemon juice
1 tbs. chopped fresh parsley
lemon wedges

Cut fish into serving pieces. Melt margarine and add pepper, lemon juice and parsley. Place fish on lightly oiled baking dish. Pour sauce over fish. Broil four inches from heat, turning once, until fish begins to flake. Garnish with lemon.

Oven-Fried Fillets

A tasty and easy way to prepare fish and without the high-fat of deep frying.

1 lb. fish fillets
2 cups cornflakes
dash ground pepper
½ tsp. garlic powder
2 tsp. chopped fresh parsley
2 tbs. vegetable oil

Rinse and dry fillets. Cut into serving pieces. Crush cornflakes in food processor. Sprinkle fish with pepper, garlic powder and chopped parsley. Dip in oil and coat with crumbs. Arrange in a single layer on a lightly oiled baking pan. Bake 10 minutes in a 500°F. oven.

Stuffed Fillet of Sole

Serve with colorful vegetables such as broccoli or green beans, carrots and cherry tomatoes. This is an easy recipe to double.

¾ lb. sole fillets
¼ lb. shrimp
½ cup white wine
¼ cup margarine
2 tbs. minced onion

½ cup sliced fresh mushrooms
¾ cup low-fat **or** nonfat milk
paprika
minced parsley

Microwave: Cut fish into serving pieces. Place a few shrimp on each piece. Roll and secure with toothpick. Coat a shallow microwave baking dish with margarine. Place stuffed fillets in baking dish. Pour wine over top. Cover with plastic wrap and microwave on High 7 to 8 minutes until fish flakes, basting with wine occasionally. Set fish aside. In a medium-size microwave-safe bowl melt margarine on High 45 seconds. Add onions and mushrooms and microwave, uncovered, on High 2 minutes. Blend in flour until smooth. Add milk, stirring until smooth. Microwave on High, uncovered, 4 to 5 minutes until thickened. Add ½ cup fish liquid from baking dish to sauce. Place fillets on microwave-safe serving platter. Pour mushroom sauce over fish. Microwave, uncovered, on Medium 3 to 4 minutes until heated through. Sprinkle with paprika and parsley.

Conventional: Place stuffed fillets in greased baking dish. Pour wine over fish and bake at 375°F., 35 to 40 minutes or until fish flakes. In saucepan, melt margarine, sauté onions and mushrooms. Add flour, stir until smooth. Add milk, stirring until thickened. After fish is cooked add ½ cup of fish liquid to sauce. Heat thoroughly. Remove fish to warm serving platter. Pour sauce over fish. Sprinkle with paprika and parsley.

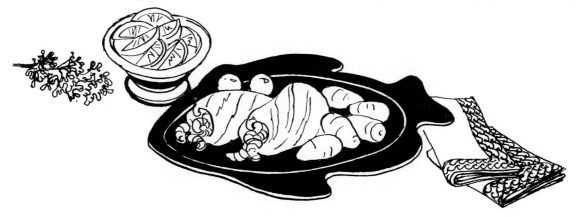

Salmon Stir-Fry

This is a quick-to-prepare, low-cholesterol dish. The vegetables stay nice and crisp.

1 can (16 ozs.) salmon
5 cups sliced vegetables—mushrooms, celery, pepper, carrots.
1 clove garlic
1 tbs. oil
water
1 tsp. cornstarch
cooked rice

Drain salmon, reserve liquid. Break salmon into chunks. Stir-fry vegetables and garlic in hot oil 1 minute. Add water to reserved salmon liquid to measure ⅓ cup. Blend in cornstarch. Stir mixture into vegetables and cook until slightly thickened. Gently stir in salmon. Heat and serve over rice.

Trout Almondine

⅓ cup margarine
4 fresh trout, 8 ozs. each
½ cup slivered blanched almonds
1½ tsp. lemon juice

Heat margarine in skillet. Sauté trout over medium heat about 5 minutes. Turn and brown on second side. Cook until fish flakes easily. Remove to heated platter. Add almonds and lemon juice to margarine in pan and cook until browned. Pour over trout.

White Clam Sauce

Clams cooked with white wine and garlic make a delicious, quick pasta sauce.

¼ cup margarine
1 large clove garlic, minced
2 tbs. flour
2 cans (6½ ozs. ea.) chopped clams
¼ cup dry white wine or vermouth
low-fat or skim milk
¼ cup parsley, finely chopped
½ tsp. thyme
salt and pepper to taste
1 lb. fresh pasta, cooked and drained

Melt margarine in small saucepan. Add garlic and cook one minute. Stir in flour and cook two minutes. Drain clams, reserving juice. Combine reserved clam juice and white wine. Add enough milk to make 2 cups liquid. Add to flour mixture gradually and cook until sauce thickens slightly. Add parsley, thyme, salt and pepper. Simmer about 10 minutes. Add clams and heat through. Serve over hot, well-drained pasta.

White Clam Sauce (page 110) ▶

Chicken

Chicken is one of America's favorite foods. We enjoy its taste and appreciate its economy. It is high in protein, B vitamins and minerals, and low in fat (if all visible fat is removed), making it one of our finest nutritional values.

The versatility of chicken is another of its assets. It can be prepared in a greater number of ways than any other meat or fish. And it lends itself perfectly to baking, broiling and barbecuing which are the preferred ways of cooking meats.

Turkey is also high in protein and low in fat. It can be substituted for chicken in many recipes—especially where cooked chicken is called for.

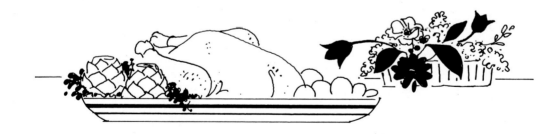

Preparation time: 10 minutes
Roasting time: 1 hour
Servings: 6

Roast Chicken

One of the easiest meals to prepare. Once the chicken is in the oven, you can forget about it except for an occasional basting. To stuff or not to stuff is a matter of choice. The Apple Stuffing (page 114) is a delicious one.

1 chicken, 3½ to 4 lbs.
pepper
tarragon
½ cup melted margarine

Wash and dry chicken. Rub inside and out with pepper and tarragon. Stuff chicken, if desired, and truss. Brush with margarine. Place on rack in a roasting pan. Roast at 450°F. about 1 hour (allow 10 more minutes if chicken is stuffed). Baste occasionally with margarine.

Preparation time: 20 minutes
Baking time: 40 minutes
Servings: 6

Apple Stuffing

This makes a delicious stuffing for the roast chicken on page 113 or a side dish with any poultry or pork.

¼ cup chopped onion
2 tbs. chopped celery
1 tbs. margarine
2 cups dry bread cubes
½ cup diced unpeeled apple
½ tsp. thyme leaves
½ tsp. crushed sage leaves
dash ground pepper
1 cup chicken broth

Cook onions and celery in margarine until tender. Combine with other ingredients. Add broth and toss to mix. Use to stuff chicken, or put in oiled baking dish. Cover and bake in 350°F. oven 40 minutes.

Preparation time: 10 minutes
Roasting time: 1 hour
Microwave: 20 minutes
Servings: 4

Roast Cornish Hens

Perfect for a small family. Serve with brown rice, a green vegetable and fruit salad.

2 (16 ozs. ea.) cornish hens, rinsed and dried
¼ cup melted margarine
½ cup water

¼ cup brandy
1 cup crushed pineapple

Conventional: Twist wing tips behind backs and tie legs together. Brush hens with margarine. Place breast side up on a rack in shallow pan. Roast uncovered in 375 °F. oven about 1 hour. Baste occasionally. Make sauce by combining water, brandy and crushed pineapple. Heat to boiling and simmer 2 minutes. Cut each hen in half and serve with sauce.

Microwave: Twist wing tips behind backs and tie legs together. Arrange breast side down on a microwave rack in baking dish. Cover with tent of oiled waxed paper. Microwave on High 8 minutes. Turn breast side up and give each hen a half turn in dish. Give dish a half turn. Cover with waxed paper. Microwave on High 6 to 8 minutes or until juices run clear. Cover tightly and let stand 3 to 5 minutes. Combine water, brandy and pineapple. Microwave 1 minute. Cut each hen in half and serve with sauce.

Preparation time: 10 minutes
Baking time: 55 minutes
Servings: 4 to 6

Lemon Chicken

Fresh lemon juice enhances the flavor of this baked chicken.

1 frying chicken, 3 lbs., cut up
2 tbs. melted margarine
3 tbs. fresh lemon juice
1 clove garlic, minced

dash ground pepper
½ tsp. salt (optional)
lemon slices

Conventional: In a small bowl combine margarine, lemon juice, garlic, pepper and salt. Place chicken in a shallow casserole dish. Pour sauce over chicken. Cover and bake in 350°F. oven about 45 minutes. Uncover and bake 10 minutes longer. Garnish with lemon slices.

Microwave: Place chicken in microwave casserole. Combine margarine, lemon, garlic, pepper and salt. Pour sauce over chicken. Microwave on High 10 to 12 minutes. Rest 5 minutes. Cook 10 minutes longer or until done and tender. Garnish with lemon.

MICROWAVE HINT: If you cover the chicken, the skin will be quite soft. If you prefer a drier skin, do not cover.

Preparation time: 15 minutes
Cooking time: 45 to 55
minutes
Servings: 4 to 6

Chicken Cacciatore

1 frying chicken, 3 lbs., cut up
2 cans (16 ozs. ea.) whole tomatoes
1 cup chopped onion
¼ cup chopped green pepper
½ cup chopped celery

½ lb. mushrooms, sliced
1 clove garlic, minced
1 tbs. fresh parsley
½ tsp. oregano
1 cup dry white wine

Trim fat from chicken. Cut hard cores from tomatoes and coarsely chop tomatoes. Brown chicken in frying pan sprayed with non-stick vegetable spray. Remove chicken from frying pan. Add onion, green pepper, celery, tomatoes, mushrooms, garlic, parsley, oregano and wine. Stir until well mixed. Return chicken to frying pan. Cover and bring to a boil. Reduce heat and simmer 45 minutes. Remove cover and increase heat. Cook until sauce reduces and thickens, about 10 minutes.

Microwave: Prepare chicken and tomatoes as above. Place chicken in 3-quart glass casserole. Cover with tomatoes, onion, pepper, celery, mushrooms, garlic, parsley, oregano and wine. Cover with waxed paper. Microwave 30 minutes. Stir occasionally. Rest 10 minutes. Mix 1 tablespoon cornstarch and 2 tablespoons water. Add to chicken and microwave 5 to 6 minutes until thickened and chicken is tender.

Preparation time: 15 minutes
Baking time: 1 hour
Microwave: 25 minutes
Servings: 4 to 6

Chicken Marengo

1 frying chicken, 3 lbs., cut up
1 can (16 ozs.) tomatoes
½ cup frozen small whole onions
1 clove garlic, minced
½ cup dry sherry

1 bay leaf
½ tsp. salt
½ tsp. thyme
¼ tsp. pepper
¼ lb. mushrooms, sliced

Trim fat and skin chicken. Place chicken in casserole dish. Remove hard cores from tomatoes and coarsely chop. In medium bowl, combine tomatoes, onions, garlic, sherry, bay leaf and seasonings. Pour over chicken. Add mushrooms. Bake, uncovered, in 375°F. oven for 1 hour. Remove bay leaf and serve.

Microwave: Place prepared chicken in microwave casserole. Combine tomatoes, onions, garlic, sherry, bay leaf and seasonings. Pour over chicken. Add mushrooms. Microwave on High 10 to 12 minutes. In small dish mix cornstarch with enough liquid to make a thin paste. Stir into casserole. Microwave 10 to 12 minutes longer. Remove bay leaf and serve.

Chicken Cacciatore (page 117) ▶

Preparation time: 20 minutes
Cooking time: 10 minutes
Servings: 4 to 6

Stir-Fried Chicken

A quick and easy dish to prepare but be sure to have everything ready before you start cooking. Vary the vegetables for a change of color and flavor. Serve with rice.

2 tbs. oil
3 chicken breast halves, skinned and
   thinly sliced
1 small onion, thinly sliced
1 carrot, thinly sliced
1 green pepper, thinly sliced
½ cup celery, sliced diagonally
1 cup sliced water chestnuts

1⅔ cups (14½ oz. can)
   chicken broth
⅓ cup dry white wine **or** an extra
   ⅓ cup broth
2 tbs. soy sauce
1 tsp. sugar
2 tbs. cornstarch
¼ cup cold water

Heat oil in heavy skillet or wok. Stir-fry chicken 2 to 3 minutes. Add onion, carrot, pepper and celery. Stir-fry 3 minutes. Stir in water chestnuts, broth, wine and soy sauce. Cook 3 minutes. Blend sugar, cornstarch and water. Add to chicken and stir until thickened. Serve over rice.

Preparation time: 5 minutes
Cooking time: 10 minutes
Servings: 4 to 6

Turkey with Orange Glaze  *Excellent*

Remember this easy dish when you're having company and there's not much time for cooking. Serve with fresh broccoli and cooked brown rice from the freezer.

1 tbs. margarine
1 lb. young turkey breast slices
2 tbs. firmly packed brown sugar
4 tsp. cornstarch
1 cup orange juice
1 tbs. lemon juice
orange slices

Melt margarine in skillet. Add turkey slices. Brown on each side. Remove to serving platter and cover. Keep warm in low oven. In skillet combine sugar and cornstarch. Add juices and stir to blend. Cook over medium heat, stirring, until glaze boils. Pour over turkey and garnish with orange slices.

Preparation time: 15 minutes
Cooking time: 10 minutes
Servings: 4 to 6

Mock Veal—Turkey *Excellent*

Quick, easy, tasty, nutritious and low-calorie! Serve with rice and a green vegetable.

1 lb. young turkey breast slices, pounded lightly
flour
1 tsp. oil
1 tsp. margarine
½ cup sliced mushrooms
1 green onion, sliced
½ tsp. thyme
½ fresh lemon
lemon slices

Dredge turkey slices in flour. Heat oil and margarine in skillet. Brown turkey. As turkey is browning add mushrooms, onion and thyme. Squeeze lemon juice over turkey slices and remove from skillet. Stir mixture remaining in skillet until blended and slightly thickened. Spoon over turkey slices. Garnish with lemon.

Meat

Meat offers these important nutrients to the diet: protein, B-vitamins, iron and zinc. It also provides most of the fat in our diets. Two-thirds of the calories in a piece of steak are fat calories. It is the fat that gives flavor to protein foods. Protein itself tastes dreadful!

Meat does NOT need to be eliminated from your diet. It is more prudent to use *lean* meats and limit portions to 3 to 4 ounces. You can reduce fat further by using an ironstone skillet for frying, spraying baking dishes with a non-stick vegetable spray (such as Pam,) and by discarding fat which accumulates in the pan as the meat browns. Remember the 4 B's—Broil, Bake, Boil or Barbeque—are better than frying.

We always recommend using lean meats. They may lack some of the flavor of higher-fat meats but the imaginative use of herbs, spices and other ingredients enhances the natural flavor.

Preparation time: 30 minutes
Cooking time: 5 minutes
Servings: 4 to 6

Barbecued Hamburgers

Serve with potato salad, a tossed green salad and sliced tomatoes.

Sauce:

1 tbs. margarine
½ cup chopped onion
¼ cup catsup
3 tbs. vinegar
1 tbs. sugar
1 tbs. Worcestershire sauce
1 tsp. paprika
1 tsp. mustard
¼ tsp. Tabasco sauce (optional)

Hamburgers:

1 lb. lean ground beef
1 cup soft bread crumbs
1 egg, lightly beaten
¼ cup minced onion
2 tbs. milk
1 tbs. prepared horseradish
½ tsp. salt
½ tsp. dry mustard

To make sauce, melt margarine in saucepan. Add onions and cook until tender. Stir in remaining ingredients and simmer 15 minutes. Gently mix hamburger ingredients and form into 6 patties. Brush patties with sauce. Broil 5 minutes on one side. Turn and broil 3 minutes on the second side.

Variations for hamburgers:

Chop onions coarsely and increase to ½ cup
Add ½ cup chopped green peppers
Add 1 cup chopped spinach
Replace bread crumbs with ¾ cup cooked rice (Porcupine patties)
Replace ½ of the ground meat with cottage cheese
Add 1 tablespoon minced parsley and ¼ cup grated Parmesan cheese

Preparation time: 30 minutes
Cooking time: 15 minutes
Servings: 8

Beef and Broccoli Stir-Fry

A 4-ounce portion contributes approximately 200 mg. sodium—not necessarily high. If you are watching sodium carefully, do not exceed your portion, or use a milder soy sauce. Serve this colorful dish with rice and sliced tomatoes.

2 tbs. dry sherry
2 tbs. soy sauce
⅓ cup water
1½ tsp. cornstarch
1 tsp. ground ginger
1 small garlic clove, minced
¼ tsp. crushed red pepper flakes
1¼ lbs. boneless round steak, cut in 2 by ¼-inch strips
1 tbs. vegetable oil
4 cups broccoli flowerets
1 cup chopped onion
½ cup mushrooms, sliced

Make marinade of sherry, soy sauce, water, cornstarch, ginger, garlic and pepper flakes. Add beef. Cover and refrigerate 30 minutes. Drain meat in colander. Reserve marinade. Heat oil in wok or large ironstone skillet on high heat. Add beef. Cook, stirring, until meat is browned on both sides. Add broccoli and onion. Fry approximately 2 more minutes. Add mushrooms, fry 1 more minute. Add marinade. Stir constantly until thickened, about 1 minute. Reheat leftovers in microwave oven.

Preparation time: 10 minutes
Cooking time: 5 to 10 minutes
Servings: 8

London Broil

A good choice for an easy company dinner because most of the preparation is made in advance. Serve with mushrooms, hot cooked rice, carrots and chilled fruit salad.

1 flank steak, about 2 lbs.
1 cup vegetable oil
½ cup wine vinegar
1 clove garlic, minced
2 tsp. Worcestershire sauce
2 tsp. dry mustard
½ tsp. salt (optional)
few drops Tabasco sauce

Remove excess fat from steak and score. Make a marinade of remaining ingredients. Mix right in a large shallow pan. Place steak in marinade. Turn steak over. Marinate, covered, in refrigerator 3 or more hours. When ready to cook, remove steak from marinade. Place on rack in broiler pan. Broil in pre-heated broiler 2 to 3 inches from heat for 3 to 4 minutes. Turn and broil 2 to 3 minutes longer. Steak should be red when sliced. Thinly slice diagonally against the grain.

London Broil (page 128) ▶

Preparation time: 10 minutes
Cooking time: 15 minutes
Servings: 6

Pepper Steak

A quick and tasty dish. Serve with brown rice, carrots and a tossed salad.

1 tbs. margarine
½ cup chopped onion
1 green pepper, cut into julienne strips
1 lb. beef round **or** sirloin tip
   cut into ⅛ by 2-inch strips
dash garlic powder
½ tsp. unsalted bouillon powder
1 cup tomatoes

1½ tsp. cornstarch
2 tbs. water
1 tbs. soy sauce
½ tsp. sugar
⅛ tsp. pepper
dash Tabasco sauce
cooked rice

Melt margarine in skillet. Sauté onion and green pepper about 2 minutes. Remove vegetables. Add beef. Sprinkle with garlic powder and sauté until browned. Stir in bouillon powder and tomatoes. Simmer 10 minutes. Blend together cornstarch, water, soy sauce, sugar, pepper and Tabasco. Stir into meat mixture and cook until thickened. Return onion and green pepper to skillet. Heat thoroughly. Spoon rice around edge of platter. Place steak and vegetables in center.

Preparation time: 15 minutes
Cooking time: 10 to 12 hours
Servings: 8

Busy Day Stew

It takes only 15 minutes to prepare this stew then it simmers in the crockery pot without being watched. Freeze half for use at a later time when you're too busy to cook. Serve with crusty French bread and minted pears.

1 lb. stew meat, cut into 1-inch pieces
4 carrots, chopped
2 celery stalks, cut in julienne strips
1 small onion, chopped
1 can (8 ozs.) tomato sauce
1½ cans (1½ cups) water

4 tbs. tapioca
1 tsp. sugar
½ tsp. salt
¼ tsp. pepper
½ tsp. garlic powder
1 cup diced potatoes

Trim all visible fat from meat and cut into 1-inch pieces. Combine all ingredients in crockery pot. Cook on low 10 to 12 hours or on high 4 to 5 hours. Or place in covered casserole and cook in 225°F. oven for 3 to 4 hours. Add potatoes during last 2 hours of cooking. Tastes even better the second day.

Preparation time: 5 minutes
Cooking time: 35 minutes
Microwave: 14 minutes
Servings: 4

Pork Chops in Apple Juice

1 tbs. vegetable oil
4 pork chops, cut 1 inch thick
1 cup apple juice

Microwave: Heat oil in skillet. Brown pork chops. Transfer to microwave-safe dish. Pour apple juice over chops. Cover with waxed paper. Microwave on High for 12 to 14 minutes or until pork chops are done.

Conventional: Heat oil in skillet. Brown pork chops. Drain off excess fat. Pour apple juice over chops. Cover and cook over low heat 35 to 40 minutes.

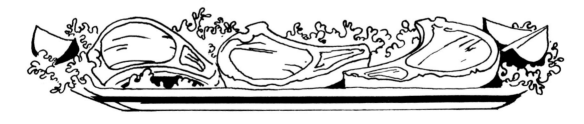

Combination Dishes

Combination dishes for the most part are meatless. They offer the color and texture of vegetables, the crunch and flavor of grains and protein in the form of dairy products and eggs.

The dairy products used in these recipes are usually low in fat, although some cheeses and eggs are utilized. In comparison with a piece of steak, these dishes provide lower fat, adequate protein and a richer source of calcium. Serve them often, especially if the members of your family are non-milk drinkers.

Combination dishes are often make-ahead dishes, too. A few minutes in the kitchen one day, can mean dinner in minutes, the next.

A freezer can play an important part in making combination dishes time-savers, too. Freeze leftover beef, pork or chicken in one-cup portions. Combined with frozen peas and rice, you have the basics for Chinese Fried Rice (page 138). Double the recipe for Marinara Sauce (page 139), freeze in one- and two-cup portions, and the time-consuming part of many combination recipes is eliminated.

Preparation time: 15 minutes
Baking time: 45 minutes
Microwave: 25 minutes
Servings: 4

Rice and Cheese Loaf

This makes a marvelous main dish. Fold in bits of leftover meats and/or vegetables before baking. Serve with green peas and sliced tomatoes.

3 eggs
2 cups nonfat milk
2 tbs. margarine, melted
1½ cups cooked rice (preferably brown)
2 cups (8 ozs.) shredded cheese
1 cup soft bread crumbs
¼ cup chopped green **or** red bell pepper
2 tbs. chopped onion
½ tsp. salt
⅛ tsp. garlic powder

Beat eggs in large bowl. Add remaining ingredients and mix well. Pour into a 1-quart baking dish coated with non-stick spray.

Oven: Bake in 325°F. oven 45 minutes.

Microwave: On Low for 25 minutes.

Preparation time: 15 minutes
Baking time: 30 minutes
Servings: 4

Broccoli-Rice Bake Dry!

A tasty and delightful meal. Serve with a cream soup, tomatoes viniagrette, French bread and fresh fruit.

1 cup chopped broccoli
¼ cup chopped onions
1½ cups cooked rice (preferably brown)
¾ cup grated cheddar cheese
3 eggs
¼ tsp. salt
¼ cup nonfat milk
⅛ tsp. pepper

Microwave onions and broccoli until barely tender or cook together in a small amount of water, or steam until barely tender. Drain well and set aside. Combine rice, half of the cheese, 1 egg, slightly beaten, and ⅛ teaspoon salt. Press evenly over bottom and sides of a 9-inch glass pie plate. Beat remaining eggs lightly. Stir in milk, pepper, salt, onion and broccoli. Spoon into crust. Bake in 375°F. oven 20 minutes. Sprinkle with remaining cheese and bake 10 minutes longer.

Preparation time: 10 minutes
Baking time: 40 minutes
Servings: 4 to 6

Fresh Vegetable Pie

Make this in a snap! Use any combination of fresh, low-calorie vegetables or bits of meat. For variety, replace Parmesan with one cup shredded cheddar cheese.

2½ cups sliced zucchini
1 cup chopped fresh tomatoes
½ cup chopped onions
¼ cup freshly grated Parmesan cheese
½ tsp. Italian seasoning
1½ cups nonfat milk
3 eggs, beaten
¾ cup biscuit mix

Mix vegetables and cheese together in a 9-inch, glass pie plate. Beat milk and eggs together. Add biscuit mix and beat until smooth. Pour over vegetables. Bake in 400°F. oven 40 minutes until golden brown. Serve immediately.

Broccoli-Rice Bake (page 135) ▶

Preparation time: 10 minutes
Cooking time: 20 minutes
Servings: 4

Chinese Fried Rice

If you have any leftover or frozen rice, try this quickie, adding whatever meat you have on hand.

3 tbs. vegetable oil
2 eggs, beaten
3 cups cold cooked rice (see page 160)
½ lb. cooked pork, chicken **or** beef, cubed
2 cups bean sprouts
1 cup **each** sliced green onions and sliced celery
1 pkg. (10 ozs.) frozen green peas, thawed
1 to 2 tbs. light soy sauce
¼ tsp. pepper

In large skillet or wok heat 1 teaspoon oil. Pour in eggs and cook without stirring until set. Turn out onto a plate. Cut into strips. Heat remaining oil until very hot. Add rice. Cook about 10 minutes, stirring frequently. Add meat, bean sprouts, green onions and celery. Stir-fry about 3 minutes. Add peas, soy sauce and pepper. Stir-fry about 2 mintues. Stir in egg strips. Serve immediately.

Preparation time: 10 minutes
Cooking time: 25 minutes
Makes: 6 cups

Marinara Sauce

This is a delicious meatless spaghetti sauce. Quadruple the recipe, cool and freeze in one- and two-cup portions to use in other recipes such as Fresh-As-Spring Fettucini, page 143, Eggplant Parmagiana, page 140, Stuffed Zucchini, page 142, or some of your own favorites.

2 tbs. olive oil
1 clove garlic, crushed
1 onion, chopped
⅓ cup celery, chopped
1 tbs. chopped fresh parsley
4 cups fresh ripe **or** canned tomatoes,
   cut in small pieces

1 can (6 ozs.) tomato paste
1 cup water
½ tsp. **each** salt, basil and oregano
¼ tsp. **each** pepper and thyme
⅛ tsp. **each** allspice and chili
   powder
1 bay leaf

Chop vegetables, except tomatoes, in food processor. Add to oil in skillet and sauté until tender. Stir in tomatoes, tomato paste and seasonings. Mix well and simmer, uncovered, at least 20 minutes, preferably 45. Remove bay leaf and serve over pasta, or freeze for later use.

Preparation time: 20 minutes
Baking time: 45 minutes
Servings: 6

Eggplant Parmagiana

Use your own defrosted Marinara Sauce and the food processor to grate the cheese for a dish that goes together in a hurry. Serve with a tossed green salad and garlic bread.

1 medium-size eggplant
¼ cup whole wheat flour
¼ tsp. salt
2 eggs, lightly beaten
¼ cup non-fat milk
1 cup fine cracker crumbs
¼ tsp. oregano
⅛ tsp. pepper
½ cup freshly grated Parmesan
1 tsp. basil
2 cups Marinara Sauce, page 139
½ pound mozzarella cheese, grated

Cut eggplant into ¼-inch slices. Combine flour and salt in one bowl. Beat eggs and milk together in another bowl. Mix crumbs, oregano and pepper, in a third bowl. Dip eggplant slices first in flour mixture, then in egg-milk mixture, then in crumbs. Layer slices with some overlap, in a 9- by 13-inch baking dish. Sprinkle each slice with Parmesan cheese and basil. Pour tomato sauce over eggplant slices. Top with mozzarella cheese. Cover tightly with aluminum foil. Bake in 350°F. oven 35 to 45 minutes until fork tender.

Preparation time: 15 minutes
Cooking time: 20 to 30
  minutes
Servings: 4

Stuffed Zucchini

Serve with pasta and a crisp green salad.

4 small zucchini
¼ cup water
½ lb. lean ground beef
2 tbs. chopped onion
1 tsp. parsley flakes

½ tsp. pepper
1 egg
1 slice bread, crumbled
3 cups Marinara Sauce, page 139
freshly grated Parmesan cheese

Place zucchini in microwave-safe dish. Add water and cover with waxed paper. Microwave on High 6 to 8 minutes, rotating dish once, until tender. Cut zucchini in half lengthwise and scoop out pulp and seeds. Discard seeds. In medium bowl combine zucchini pulp, ground beef, onion, parsley, pepper, egg and bread crumbs. Stuff each zucchini half with some of the meat mixture. Place zucchini, stuffing side up, in shallow baking dish. Spoon sauce over zucchini. Bake uncovered in 350°F. oven 30 minutes, or microwave on Medium 18 to 20 minutes. Sprinkle with Parmesan cheese.

Preparation time: 10 minutes
Cooking time: 15 minutes
Servings: 4 to 6

Fresh-As-Spring Fettucine

A light and colorful dish making best use of fresh vegetables. Alternates include green beans, green peas, asparagus and cauliflower. Serve with antipasto and French bread.

1 cup carrot slices
1 cup broccoli pieces
1 cup zucchini slices
½ cup mushroom slices
4 cups Marinara Sauce, page 139
8 ozs. fettucine **or** medium-wide noodles, cooked
½ cup freshly grated Parmesan cheese

Use food processor to slice or chop vegetables. Add vegetables to marinara sauce. Bring to boil over medium heat. Immediately reduce heat and simmer until vegetables are crisp tender, approximately 15 minutes. Serve sauce over hot cooked noodles. Garnish with Parmesan cheese. Sauce reheats well.

Legumes—Dried Beans, Peas and Lentils
PROTEIN COMPLEMENTS

Dried beans and peas are a part of every culture. No wonder—they are tasty, inexpensive and nutritious. Although they are an incomplete protein they combine with almost any other food—another protein, milk, grain, seeds, nuts or a vegetable—to produce a "complete" protein.

You must consume "complete" protein within the same meal for your body to receive the full value from the protein you eat. Most animal proteins are "complete"— most vegetable proteins are "incomplete." (See chart on page 146.) Two or more incomplete proteins can be combined in a meal to complement each other and form a complete protein. Nearly all vegetables contain some protein.

Any one of the combinations shown on the chart on page 147 will give you high quality protein. By eating more vegetable protein you will add fiber, vitamins and minerals to your meal plan, while reducing fat and cholesterol as you cut down on animal protein.

◀ **Pirate's Surprise (page 150)**

"Incomplete" Proteins Plus Complements Equal "Complete" Proteins

If you combine vegetable proteins in the same meal in any of the ways suggested below, you will obtain complete protein equivalent to the protein in meat and other animal foods.

INCOMPLETE PROTEIN	+ COMPLEMENT	= COMPLETE PROTEIN (examples of possible combinations)
Cereals	+ Milk	Oatmeal with Milk
Cereals	+ Eggs	Bread Pudding (page 179)
Cereals	+ Cheese	Rice and Cheese Loaf (page 135)
Cereals	+ Nuts	Rice or Bulgur Pilaf with Almonds (page 162)
Cereals	+ Seeds	Cereal Combo (page 59)
Legumes	+ Cereals	Lentils Creole with Noodles (page 152)
Legumes	+ Cheese	Italian Beans (page 151)
Legumes	+ Seeds	Tofu Patties (page 154)
Legumes	+ Vegetables	Pirate's Surprise (page 150)
Leafy Green Vegetables	+ Seeds, Eggs	Spinach Salad with Eggs and Seeds

Examples of "Incomplete" Proteins

CEREALS

barley	pasta
brown rice	rye
bulgur wheat	tritacale
cornmeal	wheat
oats	wild rice

LEGUMES

black beans	mung beans
black-eyed peas	peas
garbanzo beans	peanuts
kidney beans	pinto beans
lentils	red beans
lima beans	soy beans

SEEDS

poppy
pumpkin
sunflower
sesame

NUTS

almonds
cashews
pecans
pinenuts
walnuts

COOKING DRIED BEANS, PEAS AND LENTILS

Most legumes require a soaking period and long, slow cooking (lentils and split peas are exceptions). You can speed the process by using the quick-soak method: Add 3 parts water to 1 part beans; bring to a full boil and boil for two minutes. Remove from heat, cover and let stand for 1 hour. Drain and freeze without cooking. When ready to cook the frozen beans, defrost by running cold water over them and cook as usual, except the cooking time will be shorter—between 30 and 60 minutes.

Beans can also be cooked all day in a crockery pot or in a 225 °F. oven. Add lemon juice, vinegar, sugar or tomato sauce only after the beans are done. Acid foods tend to toughen the beans and increase cooking time.

Canned beans are quick, but have the disadvantage of salt added to the broth. To reduce the salt, discard the broth and rinse the beans under cold running water. Remember to reduce any other salt called for in the recipe.

The easiest way to have nourishing beans on hand for tasty and quick dishes is to precook them as previously described and freeze in one- or 2-cup portions in air-tight freezer containers. (Be sure to label and date.) The recipes in this section assume you have frozen, cooked or canned beans on hand.

Tasty Bean Spread

Any leftover beans can be used to make this delightful spread for crackers, to stuff celery or even for a robust sandwich. The color of the spread will depend on the beans you use. If it needs a little garnishing, sprinkle with chopped fresh tomatoes and cilantro.

1 cup cooked kidney, pinto **or** garbanzo beans
2 tbs. vegetable oil
1 to 2 tbs. finely chopped green onions
1 tsp. finely chopped fresh cilantro **or** parsley
1 tsp. lemon juice
⅛ tsp. salt
dash Tabasco sauce

Place beans in food processor bowl and process to a smooth paste. Add remaining ingredients. Process until smooth. Chill thoroughly.

Preparation time: 10 minutes
Baking time: 20 minutes
Servings: 6

Pirate's Surprise

An eye-appealing assortment of colors and shapes. Serve piping hot in bowls accompanied by crusty French bread and a crisp green salad.

1 onion, chopped
1 green pepper, cut into strips
½ cup diced celery
2 garlic cloves, minced
1 can (16 ozs.) whole kernel corn, drained
3 cups cooked kidney beans, drained

1 can (16 ozs.) tomatoes
1 tbs. Worcestershire sauce
1 tsp. oregano
½ tsp. thyme
⅔ cup shredded cheese

Use food processor to prepare vegetables. Cook onion, pepper, celery and garlic in small amount of water until tender. Drain well. Combine with remaining ingredients, except cheese. Break tomatoes into smaller pieces with spoon. Place in a 2-quart casserole or Dutch oven. Sprinkle cheese on top. Cover dish and bake in 350°F. oven 25 to 30 minutes, or microwave on High for 7 minutes. (Uncover dish if you wish a thicker mixture.) Leftovers reheat well.

Preparation time: 15 minutes
Cooking time: 30 minutes
Servings: 4

Italian Beans

Quick to prepare if beans are cooked ahead and ready to use (see page 148).

¾ cup onion, chopped
1 clove garlic, minced
1 tbs. vegetable oil
3 ozs. medium-wide noodles, cooked and drained
2 cups cooked white beans, defrosted if frozen
1 can (14½ ozs.) tomatoes
   or 1¾ cup undrained whole tomatoes, diced
1 cup (4 ozs.) shredded mozzarella cheese
½ tsp. salt
½ tsp. oregano
dash pepper
¼ cup grated Parmesan cheese

Sauté onion and garlic in oil in small skillet. Combine remaining ingredients, except Parmesan cheese, in 1½-quart baking dish. Sprinkle with Parmesan. Bake in 350°F. oven 30 minutes or microwave on High 10 minutes or until bubbly.

Preparation time: 10 minutes
Cooking time: 30 minutes
Servings: 4

Lentils Creole

A tasty lentil dish. Cayenne or pepper sauce are used for added spice. Serve with brown rice or noodles, corn and pickled cucumbers.

⅓ cup onion, chopped
1 green **or** red pepper, chopped finely
1 tbs. vegetable oil
1 cup cooked **or** canned tomatoes
¼ tsp. sugar
⅛ tsp. freshly ground black pepper
⅛ tsp. cayenne **or** dash pepper sauce (optional)
1 cup cooked lentils

Chop onion and green pepper in food processor. Heat oil in frying pan. Add onion and green pepper. Cook slowly until soft. Add tomatoes, sugar, and cayenne pepper. Break up tomatoes with spoon. Stir in lentils. Simmer 30 minutes.

Chalupes (page 157) ▶

Tofu Patties

Tofu has a rather bland taste which is complemented by herbs and spices. You can vary the patties by: adding a slice of cheddar after browning patties, and broiling until melted; or serving with a spaghetti sauce; or serving with a white sauce to which you've added mustard or herbs. A complete meal might be: Tofu patties, baked potato, green beans, sliced tomatoes and cucumbers and fresh fruit.

1 carton (about 16 ozs.) tofu
½ cup **each** finely chopped celery,
   green pepper and onion
1 clove garlic, minced
1 tbs. vegetable oil
1 egg, beaten

½ cup whole wheat flour
2 tbs. Worcestershire sauce
2 tbs. curry powder
½ tsp. salt
sesame seeds

Drain tofu in strainer (be sure most of liquid is removed) and mash. Use food processor to chop vegetables. Sauté vegetables in oil until soft. Add vegetables and remaining ingredients, except sesame seeds, to mashed tofu. Form mixture into patties. Coat with sesame seeds. Brown in ironstone or other non-stick skillet. Freeze extra patties for later use.

Preparation time: 10 minutes
Cooking time: 10 hours
Servings: 4 to 6

Spicy Beans

A delicious bean dish. To make a tasty burrito filling use less water or cook uncovered until thickened. The flavor is even better when beans are reheated.

1 cup red kidney beans
1 small fresh pork hock, all fat removed
1 onion, chopped
4 small dried red peppers, finely chopped **or** red pepper sauce, to taste
¼ tsp. salt
¼ tsp. garlic powder
⅛ tsp. cumin

Soak beans several hours or overnight. Drain and rinse beans. Add 1½ cups fresh water and remaining ingredients. Slow cook in crock pot 10 to 12 hours or in 225 °F. oven 6 to 8 hours.

Preparation time: 10 minutes
Cooking time: 45 minutes
Servings: 6 to 8

Chili

1 lb. lean ground turkey, beef **or** veal
1 onion, chopped
1 cup fresh tomatoes **or** 1 can
  (7½ ozs.) tomatoes
1 can (8 ozs.) tomato purée
1 cup water

2 cups cooked or canned kidney
  beans, drained
2 tsp. chili powder
¼ tsp. salt (optional)
½ tsp. **each** garlic powder, oregano
  and ground cumin
¼ tsp. pepper

Break up meat and cook in large non-stick skillet until no pink remains. Drain off fat. Add remaining ingredients. Bring to boiling and reduce heat. Cover and simmer 45 minutes or slow cook in a crock pot, or in a 225 °F. oven 6 to 8 hours. Slow cooking develops flavor in chili, but this chili turns out surprisingly well when quickly made in a microwave oven. Leftovers are even better after being reheated.

Microwave: Break meat into a round microwave-safe dish. Microwave on High 5 minutes. Drain off fat. Add remaining ingredients except beans. Microwave covered, 10 minutes. Add beans and stir. Microwave 3 minutes.

Preparation time: 10 minutes
Cooking time: 35 minutes
Makes: 8 to 10

Chalupas

Adding shredded lettuce turns these into tostadas. Serve with slices of crisp jicama and cold milk.

½ lb. lean ground beef **or** 1 cup leftover cooked meat, cubed
½ onion, chopped
1½ tsp. chili powder
½ tsp. cumin powder
⅛ tsp. pepper
1 cup cooked pinto beans, mashed
8 to 10 corn tortillas
½ cup (2 ozs.) mozzarella cheese, grated
1 to 2 fresh tomatoes, diced

Use food processor to chop onion, grate cheese and mash beans. Brown beef and onion in frying pan. Drain off fat. Stir in spices and beans. Simmer, covered, for 30 minutes. Stir occasionally to prevent sticking. Five to seven minutes before serving, lay corn tortillas on racks in 350°F. oven. Heat until crisp. Spread meat-bean mixture on warm tortillas. Sprinkle with cheese and top with tomatoes.

Grains and Breads

America is rediscovering grains! For many years consumption of refined flour, sugar and fat-ladened foods has continued to escalate. At the same time, so called experts decried carbohydrates as fat-making monsters!

With increased emphasis on nutrition and fiber in foods, whole grains are now winning applause as life-giving marvels. Popular items include whole grain breads, whole wheat pancakes and muffins that can be loaded with nuts, seeds, shredded vegetables and dried fruits, pita bread and tabbouli salad (page 84).

Contrary to popular opinion, white bread, white rice and pasta are NOT non-nutritious lumps of matter. These foods contain a similar level of complex carbohydrate, protein, vitamins and minerals to that of whole grains. The extra pluses of whole grains are the taste and the fiber. Choose more whole grains, but do not feel guilty eating your favorite sourdough!

Whole grains add a marvelous nutty taste and texture to foods. Because one must chew more, eating speed is reduced. Whole grains offer a feeling of satisfaction and satiety that helps prevent overeating.

Brown rice does take somewhat longer to cook, but its flavor and texture are superior to white rice. To save time, cook several batches for the freezer. Measure out one- or two-cup portions and freeze in zip-loc bags or freezer containers. Defrost when needed for rice pilaf, rice salads or hot cooked rice to go with stir-fried beef or chicken. Add it to chicken broth for quick chicken rice soup or use it in combination dishes such as Broccoli Rice Bake (page 135) and Rice and Cheese Loaf (page 134).

Bulgur is another grain worth knowing. It is wheat that has been parboiled, dried and cracked and is a favorite of the Middle Eastern countries. A pleasant alternative to rice, it is easy and fast to prepare and is rich in iron, calcium, and B vitamins—especially niacin, riboflavin and thiamine.

Cooking time: 55 minutes
Makes: 3 cups

Brown Rice

Next to wheat, rice is the world's most widely grown grain for food. Whole grain brown rice retains all the original nutrients of the rice kernel.

2 cups water or chicken broth
1 cup brown rice
½ tsp. salt (optional)

Bring water to a full, rolling boil in a heavy saucepan with a lid. Add rice slowly so water does not stop boiling. Bring to a full boil, cover pan and reduce heat to low. Cook about 55 minutes or until rice is tender and liquid absorbed. Remove from heat and let stand five minutes. Serve immediately or cool and refrigerate, covered, or freeze in airtight freezer bags or containers.

Rice and Cheese Loaf (page 134) ▶

Bulgur Pilaf

Bulgur is rich in iron, calcium, B vitamins and potassium.

1 tbs. margarine
1 small onion, chopped
1 cup uncooked bulgur
2 cups broth or water
½ tsp. salt
freshly ground pepper, to taste

Melt margarine in saucepan over medium heat. Add onion and sauté until it is limp. Add bulgur and cook, stirring, a minute or two. Add broth, salt and pepper. Bring to boil and reduce heat. Cover and simmer 15 minutes until liquid is absorbed.

Variations
- Add toasted nuts to pilaf just before serving.
- Substitute brown rice for bulgur. Cook 45 to 60 minutes until rice is done and liquid is absorbed.
- Sauté ½ cup sliced mushrooms along with onion. Add bulgur or brown rice and continue as directed.

Preparation time: 5 minutes
Cooking time: 50 minutes
Servings: 6

Fruited Barley Soup

A simple Dutch recipe from my childhood. We ate it as a dessert, either hot or cold. Any meal lacking a starch dish (meat and 2 vegetables, for example) would be completed by adding this tasty and easy dish. Leftover fruits or dried fruits lend themselves well.

1 cup barley
5 cups water
¼ tsp. salt
½ to 1 cup fruit (raisins, prunes, apricots, peaches)
1 tbs. brown sugar
1 to 2 tsp. lemon juice

Soak barley in 3 cups water overnight. When ready to cook barley add remaining 2 cups water and salt. Bring to boil, cover and simmer 45 minutes. Add fruit and simmer 5 minutes or until soft. Just before serving add brown sugar and lemon juice.

Wheat Light Pancakes

Pancakes can be a quick and delicious dinner. Serve with Canadian bacon and a fruit salad. Encourage family members to use a lighter hand with butter and syrup. For crepes, add 1 egg and ½ cup nonfat milk to pancake recipe and mix in blender until smooth.

½ cup whole wheat flour
½ cup all-purpose flour
1 tbs. baking powder
¼ tsp. salt
1 egg, beaten
1 cup nonfat milk
1 tbs. vegetable oil
½ tsp. vanilla

Stir together dry ingredients and make well in center. Combine egg, milk, oil and vanilla. Add to dry ingredients. Stir just until moistened (batter will be lumpy). Bake on hot ironstone griddle or skillet.

Ever-Ready Bran Muffins

These tender bran muffins can be baked fresh each morning in your microwave or conventional oven.

3 cups Bran Buds, **or** All Bran cereal
2½ cups all-purpose flour
¾ cup sugar
2½ tsp. baking soda
½ tsp. salt

2 eggs, beaten
½ cup vegetable oil
2 cups buttermilk
1 cup nuts **or** raisins **or** dates

Combine dry ingredients in bowl and make a well in center. Beat eggs. Add oil and milk. Pour liquid ingredients into dry ingredients and mix just until moistened (there will be some lumps). Add fruits at baking time. Cover container and store in refrigerator. Batter will keep for several weeks. When ready to bake fill muffin cups ⅔ full. Fruit can be placed in bottoms of muffin cups, if desired.

Microwave: 3 minutes on High for 6 muffins or until tops are dry.

Oven: Bake at 400°F. for 15 to 20 minutes.

Nutri-Muffins

Kids love these. Fresh strawberries or grapefruit sections, two muffins and a glass of milk make a nutritious breakfast. If time is limited, assemble and measure the ingredients in advance. The mixing and baking go fast and you'll be rewarded with three dozen delicious muffins which freeze well. A food processor is very handy when making this recipe.

1 cup whole wheat flour
1 cup white flour
⅔ cup instant nonfat dry milk
½ cup brown sugar
⅓ cup wheat germ
2 tsp. baking powder
½ tsp. **each** salt and baking soda
½ cup unsalted roasted peanuts
¼ cup walnuts, pecans **or** almonds

½ cup dried apricots
½ cup raisins
3 eggs
½ cup oil
⅓ cup molasses
2 bananas, mashed **or** 1 cup grated carrots **or** zucchini
¾ cup orange juice

Combine dry ingredients. Use food processor to chop nuts and apricots. Mix dry ingredients, nuts, apricots and raisins together in large mixing bowl. Blend thoroughly to prevent large lumps. Beat eggs in food processor until foamy. Add oil, molasses, orange juice and bananas in order given. Process after each addition. Pour liquid ingredients into dry ingredients in mixing bowl. Mix with wooden spoon just until moistened. Spray muffin cups with non-stick spray. Fill cups ¾ full with batter. Bake at 350°F. for 20 minutes.

Note: Batter can be baked in two 9 × 5 × 3-inch loaf pans, at 350°F. for 1 hour.

Zucchini Nut Muffins

These tasty nutritious muffins keep well and freeze well. Pull from the freezer and add to child's lunch pail. Or, prepare a cream cheese frosting and serve to guests as a dessert.

2 eggs
⅓ cup firmly-packed brown sugar
⅓ cup honey
½ cup margarine, melted
1 tsp. vanilla
1¾ cups flour (part whole wheat)

1 tsp. **each** salt and baking soda
½ tsp. **each** baking powder and nutmeg
1½ tsp. cinnamon
1 cup oats
½ cup nuts **or** raisins **or** dates
2 cups shredded zucchini

Beat eggs lightly. Blend in sugar, honey, melted margarine and vanilla. Stir dry ingredients together. Add to egg mixture and stir until just moistened. Quickly and gently stir in oats, fruit, nuts and zucchini. Spoon into muffin pans.

Microwave: On High 3 minutes for 6 muffins or until tops are dry.

Oven: Bake in 350°F. oven for 25 minutes.

Preparation time: 15 minutes
Baking time: 45 minutes
Makes: 1 loaf

Banana Nut Bread

A rich-tasting loaf your family will love. While you're at it, bake an extra loaf for the freezer. Slice and serve for breakfast or as a lunch box "treat."

2 cups whole wheat flour
2½ tsp. baking powder
½ tsp. soda
½ tsp. salt
½ cup margarine, softened

1 cup sugar
1 egg
½ cup buttermilk **or** sour milk
1 cup mashed banana
½ cup chopped walnuts

Stir dry ingredients together. Cream margarine and sugar together. Add egg and beat until fluffy. Add dry ingredients alternately with buttermilk and bananas beating until smooth after each addition. Pour batter into a 9 × 5 × 3-inch loaf pan sprayed with non-stick spray. If using a metal pan, bake in 350°F. oven 35 to 40 minutes. If pan is glass, bake in 325°F. oven 45 minutes. To test for doneness, insert wooden pick in center. If it comes out clean, the bread is done. Remove from pan and cool on wire rack.

Preparation time: 15 minutes
Baking time: 30 minutes
Makes: 16 2 × 2-in. pieces or
18 muffins

Cornbread

Cornbread is always the right accompaniment to dried bean and pea dishes. Serve it hot, right out of the oven. Leftovers can be warmed in the microwave nicely. Try cornbread wth eggs for breakfast!

1½ cups yellow cornmeal
1½ cups sifted flour
1 tbs. baking powder
¼ tsp. salt

¼ cup sugar
½ cup vegetable oil
2 eggs, beaten
1¼ cup skim milk

Sift dry ingredients into medium-size mixing bowl. Blend beaten eggs and oil; add milk. Add liquid ingredients to dry ingredients and stir until just blended. Pour into an 8 by 8-inch pan which has been sprayed with a non-stick spray. Bake in 400°F. oven for 30 minutes **or** spoon batter into microwave-safe muffin tins and microwave on High 3 minutes for 6 muffins or until tops are dry. The size of this recipe requires microwaving in 3 batches.

Corn and Lima Salad (page 82)
◀ **Cornbread (page 171)**
Chili (page 156)

Desserts

Desserts are usually thought to be full of calories. They need not be. The following selection of recipes are lower in calories and saturated fat because we've chosen to use polyunsaturated oils or margarine, less sugar, nonfat or low-fat milk and fewer eggs. You can adapt your own favorite dessert recipes by following the same methods.

Simple Desserts

Fresh fruit served plain is always an easy dessert, but at times when a bit more is wanted, try one of the following:

- Top vanilla yogurt with granola.
- Sprinkle grapefruit halves with ½ teaspoon brown sugar and broil 3 to 4 minutes. Serve hot.
- Make a parfait with unsweetened applesauce and low-fat cottage cheese. Top with cinnamon sugar.
- Mix raisins and chopped nuts and sprinkle over ice milk or plain yogurt.
- Spread apple slices with peanut butter.
- Serve fresh fruit such as grapes, pears, apples, ripe bananas with cheese.
- Spoon plain yogurt over fresh peaches, apricots or nectarines. Drizzle a little honey over the top.

Yogurt Treats

Fresh fruits or fruit juices blended with plain yogurt makes a delicious, lower-in-calories dessert or snack. Yogurt provides protein, calcium and other minerals, and vitamins. Try freezing your favorite yogurt in 4-ounce paper cups for a quick snack.

Strawberry Drink

1 cup plain yogurt
¾ cup milk

1 pkg. (10 ozs.) frozen strawberries
(use fresh in season)

Combine ingredients in blender container. Blend on high until smooth.

Fruit Juice Yogurt

2 tbs. frozen juice (orange, apple, grape) concentrate, **undiluted**
1 cup plain yogurt

Stir fruit juice concentrate into yogurt. Chill or serve immediately.

Preparation time: 15 to 20 minutes

Servings: 4 to 6

Minted Fruit Fondue

This pretty dessert can also be served as a party dip or fruit salad.

1 banana, sliced
1 unpeeled apple, cut into chunks
1 unpeeled pear, cut into chunks
3 tbs. lemon juice
1 cup orange juice
1 tbs. cornstarch
⅛ tsp. mint extract

Toss fruits with lemon juice. Arrange on platter. In small sauce pan, combine orange juice, cornstarch and mint extract. Cook over medium heat, stirring constantly, until thickened and bubbly. Pour into fondue pot set over low heat. Serve fruit with fondue forks or bamboo skewers. Dip fruit into sauce.

Variation

Place fruits in parfait glasses and spoon sauce over fruit. Garnish with mint leaves.

Grapes Aloha

Fragrant fresh pineapple and grapes make a refreshing dessert.

1 tbs. brown sugar
dash nutmeg
1 cup plain low-fat yogurt
1½ cups seedless grapes
1 large ripe fresh pineapple

Gently combine sugar, nutmeg and yogurt. Fold in grapes and chill. Peel pineapple and cut into 6 slices, about ¾ inch thick. Core and chill. To serve, place pineapple on chilled dessert plates and cut through into bite-size pieces, but leave rings intact. Top each with ¼ cup grape mixture.

Minted Fruit Fondue (page 175) ▶

Preparation time: 15 minutes
Freezing time: 2 hours
Servings: 4

Strawberry Ice

A tasty, low-fat ending to a heavy meal or a light summer snack.

4 cups fresh strawberries
1½ tsp. lemon juice
1 tbs. honey **or** sugar

Place all ingredients in food processor bowl and purée. Pour into shallow pan. Cover and freeze until solid. Remove from freezer and process until mixture is slushy. Pour into bowl, cover and freeze. Soften slightly before spooning into serving dishes.

Preparation time: 15 minutes
Baking time: 45 minutes
Servings: 6

New-Fashioned Bread Pudding

A great way to get extra milk in your family's diet. Milk provides us with calcium, protein and vitamins A and D.

2 eggs
⅔ cup sugar
¼ tsp. salt (optional)
½ tsp. vanilla
3 cups hot low-fat or nonfat milk

1 tbs. margarine
1¼ cups broken pieces of bread
½ cup raisins or chopped nuts
cinnamon

Beat eggs, sugar, salt and vanilla together. Add hot milk and margarine. Beat until blended. Spread bread and raisins in bottom of a 1½-quart casserole. Add custard mixture. Stir gently to mix. Sprinkle with cinnamon. Set in shallow pan on oven rack. Pour hot water into pan to a depth of 1 inch. Bake in 350°F. oven 40 to 45 minutes or until knife inserted near center comes out clean.

Preparation time: 15 minutes
Baking time: 35 minutes
Microwave: 12 minutes
Servings: 6

Easiest Apple Betty

This version of an old favorite uses whole wheat bread slices for faster preparation and better flavor. The layers are very pretty when served.

¾ cup sugar	6 slices whole wheat bread
1 tsp. cinnamon	4 to 6 medium-size tart apples, peeled and sliced
½ tsp. nutmeg	1 cup light cream or milk (optional)
6 tsp. margarine	½ tsp. nutmeg

Spray a 3-quart casserole dish with non-stick spray. In small bowl, mix sugar, cinnamon and nutmeg. Spread margarine on bread. Place ⅓ of apples in casserole. Top with 2 slices of bread. Sprinkle with sugar mixture. Repeat layers twice. Cover with foil. Bake in 400°F. oven for 30 minutes. Stir and bake, uncovered, 5 minutes. Serve with light cream or milk and a sprinkle of nutmeg.

Microwave: Follow conventional directions for layering apples, bread and sugar mixture. Cover with plastic wrap. Microwave on High 8 minutes. Stir gently to push apples on the outside toward the center. Give dish a half turn . Microwave 4 minutes longer. Allow 2 to 3 minutes standing time before serving.

Preparation time: 15 minutes
Microwave: 12 minutes
Servings: 6

Microwave Apple Crisp

4 cups sliced, peeled apples
2 tbs. lemon juice
½ cup quick-cooking oats
¼ cup whole wheat flour
½ cup brown sugar
6 tbs. margarine
½ tsp. cinnamon
¼ tsp. nutmeg

Place apples in a microwave-safe 9-inch pie plate. Sprinkle with lemon juice. Cover and microwave on High 2 minutes. Combine remaining ingredients in microwave-safe bowl. Microwave on High 2 minutes, stirring after 1 minute. Sprinkle over apples. Microwave, uncovered, on High 8 minutes or until apples are tender. Leftovers are delicious reheated.

Preparation time: 10 minutes
Baking time: 10 to 15 minutes
Makes: 60 cookies

Oatmeal Raisin Cookies

These are a favorite for the lunch box and are wonderful with a glass of cold milk for an afternoon snack.

½ cup margarine
1½ cups brown sugar
2 eggs
½ cup nonfat milk
2 cups flour
1 tsp. vanilla

½ tsp. soda
1 tsp. baking powder
1 tsp. salt
1 tsp. cinnamon
2½ cups oats
1 cup raisins

Insert steel blade in food processor bowl. Add margarine and brown sugar. Process until light and fluffy, about 30 seconds. Add eggs, milk and vanilla. Process on and off until blended. Combine flour, soda, baking powder, salt and cinnamon. Add to creamed mixture and process just until blended. Stir in oats and raisins by hand. Drop by spoonfuls onto cookie sheets. Bake in 350°F. oven for 10 to 12 minutes.

Preparation time: 15 minutes
Baking time: 60 minutes
Microwave: 12 minutes
Makes: 1 cake

Pumpkin Spice Cake

1 cup whole wheat flour
1 cup all-purpose flour
2 tsp. baking powder
1 tsp. baking soda
½ tsp. salt
¼ tsp. **each** nutmeg and cloves

1¼ cups sugar
4 eggs
2 cups (16-oz. can) pumpkin
¾ cup unsweetened applesauce
¼ cup vegetable oil
1 cup bran cereal

Grease and flour an 8-cup bundt pan. In medium bowl, mix flours, baking powder, soda, salt, cloves, ginger and sugar. In large bowl beat eggs using electric mixer. Add pumpkin, applesauce, oil and cereal. Mix 3 minutes until cereal is moist. On low speed add flour. Mix until just moistened. Pour batter into prepared pan. Bake in 350°F. oven 60 to 65 minutes or until toothpick inserted in center of cake comes out clean. Remove from oven and cool on rack 30 minutes before removing from pan. Cool completely.

Microwave: Pour batter into prepared microwave bundt pan. Microwave on Medium for 11 to 12 minutes or until toothpick inserted in center of cake comes out clean. Allow cake to cool 5 to 10 minutes before removing from pan. Dust with powdered sugar if desired.

Menu Suggestions

We've put together some menu suggestions incorporating recipes in this cookbook. We've utilized foods that can be made ahead (soup stock, rice, muffins) and frozen and then pulled from your freezer to make a quick lunch or dinner.

Tossed Green Salad / Herb Dressing
Spicy Beans
Cornbread   Margarine
Microwave Apple Crisp

Pickled Beets
Rice and Cheese Loaf
Broccoli with Lemon Sauce
Apple Betty

Mushrooms Parmesan
Pork Chops in Apple Juice
Corn and Lima Salad   Sliced Tomatoes
Banana Nut Bread

Quick Potato Soup
Main Dish Salad with Turkey Strips
Zucchini Nut Muffins
Strawberry Ice

Microwave's Marvelous Fish
Baked Potato/Glorified Margarine
Stir-Fry Vegetable Medley
Pumpkin Spice Cake

Roast Chicken/Apple Dressing
Broccoli with Lemon Sauce
Whole Wheat Biscuits
Minted Fruit Fondue

Minestrone Soup/Crusty French Bread
Tossed Green Salad/Herb Dressing
Fruit and Cheese

London Broil
Marinated Raw Vegetable Salad
Baked Potato with Chives
Fresh Fruit Cup

Tossed Green Salad/Yogurt Dressing
Mock Veal—Turkey
Brown Rice   Orange Carrots
Oatmeal Raisin Cookies

Lentil Soup
Peachy Chicken Salad
Ever-Ready Bran Muffins

Index

Vegetables *continued*

Strawberry Ice (page 178)